Illustrated
of
Wildlife
found in
Northamptonshire

The Earth is billions of years old
Energy matter and radiation equals +
Energy in gravitation equals −
Overall energy of the universe equals nil
Therefore the universe emerged out of nothing
and remains for all time

NATURE

One lesson, nature, let me learn of thee, one lesson, that in every wind is blown. One lesson of two duties served in one through the loud world proclaim their enmity – of toil unserved from tranquillity, of labour that is still advance outgrows far noiser schemes, accomplished in repose, too great for haste, too high for rivalry.

Yes; while on earth a thousand discords ring man senseless uproar mingling with his toil, still do they sleepless minsters move on, their glorious tasks in silence perfecting; still working, blaming still our vain turmoil labourer's that shall not fail, when man is gone.

Matthew Arnold
(1822-1888)

COUNTY LOCATION

NORTHAMPTONSHIRE

FOREWORD

The wonderful thing about observing the natural world is that it can be enjoyed by both the young and old has no colour or class barriers. Each new day brings with it a new experience, from seeing the sky changing each second, landscapes changing with each ray of light to seeing each season having it's time to display its own glories.

In the case of man's creations when magnified they become increasingly cruder, where as in nature we see increasing beauty, even in the most mundane of nature's subjects.

Having spent 40+ years both observing and photographing nature, I feel very privileged to have been able to record a very small number of nature's subjects over this period.

The one special picture in this book for me is that of the female Blackbird as it reminds me of her trust as a wild bird in letting me come within touching distance of her, each day that I fed the birds in my garden. These were truly wonderful moments.

I have produced this book to show the reader a very small snapshot of the wildlife that can be found it the county, and hope that they will enjoy seeing the wildlife, as much as I have enjoyed recording it.

DL

So take time to stop and stare, observe the beauty of the sky, be drawn into the landscape, and receive the inner peace that nature gives.

DL

Illustrated Book
of
Wildlife
found in
Northamptonshire

INDEX

NORTHAMPTONSHIRE

Northamptonshire lies across the Heart of England, is about 75 miles in length with a width of about 26 miles. It runs diagonally from North West to South West. The county has a distinctive character with many Ironstone villages being made from the Ironstone Quarries of the North of the county. It is nationally known for its squires and spires having many country houses and churches set amongst the rolling countryside.

The climate is average, moderately extreme in terms of temperature, with a generally moderate rainfall, with less sunshine than average. The warmest months generally occurring in July – August, the coldest months being January and February. The county receives on average 630mm (24.8") of rainfall a year, which is below the UK's average of 1000mm (39.3").

The prevailing wind for the county is from the South West, with the county getting its fair share of gales from time to time.

The county has a great variety of older sedimentary rocks and younger superficial deposits, which give it an intricate pattern of different types of soil, and therefore a wide range of habitats for nature.

The hills within the county are small and no more than 150m (495ft) above sea level.

HABITATS

THE TYPE OF HABITATS WHERE YOU ARE LIKELY TO FIND
THE WILDLIFE OF THE COUNTY.

UNIMPROVED MEADOWS

These have declined since the Second World War. Many types of flowers can be encountered on this type of habitat, including Bird's-Foot Trefoil, Salad Burnet, Hedge Bedstraw, Bell Flower, Common Knapweed, Buttercups, etc.

ANCIENT WOODLAND

Most ancient woodlands are found in the North of the county, Yardley Chase, Salcey Forest Whittlewood. Flowers such as Wood Anemone, Nettle-Leaved Bell Flower, Yellow Archangel, Herb-Paris, Orchids, Early Purple, Greater Butterfly, Wood Sorrel, Lilly-of-the-Valley, can still be found in the remaining woods.

HEATHLAND

This type of habitat is not common in the county. Harlestone Firs near Northampton is the best site for acid loving plants, such as Harebell, Broom, Tormentil, Bell Heather and the now rare Petty Whin.

ROADSIDE HEDGES

Hedges go back as far as one can remember and have formed part of our countryside for centuries. They form an important habitat for our mammals and birds, and the older hedgerows have a number of useful shrubs including Blackthorn, Field Maple, Guelder Rose, Wayfaring Tree, Wild Cherry, Elder, Buckthorn and Wild Roses.

WATERWAYS AND STREAMS

Rivers and streams form an important habitat in the county. Recently the water quality has improved and this in turn has seen an increase in the wildlife seen along the banks including aquatic plants and animals associated with water.

OLD PONDS AND DITCHES

In many cases these are slow moving or stagnant fresh water ponds which are ideal for aquatic plants including the Water-Lilies, Perennial Herbs such as the Rigid Hornwort. This cover is suitable for Frogs, Toads and Newts including the endangered Great-Crested Newt.

QUARRIES

Much of Northamptonshire has been subjected to Quarrying over a long period. Quarries have very poor soils and therefore do not have the very vigorous plants. You can find: Bird's-Foot Trefoil, smaller Grasses, Wild Strawberry, Blue Fleabane, Common Centaury, Bee Orchids and many Thistles including The Woolly.

NATURE RESERVES

Over the last few years, we have seen a number of new sites, including Summer Leys Meadows and Stanwick Lakes along with the more established ones. These have been established to preserve and increase the county's flora and fauna for future generations to enjoy, and will play a major role in keeping our wildlife safe and unspoilt.

RED KITE

NORTHAMPTONSHIRE REINTRODUCTION PROJECT SUCCESS.

Derek Henderson (DJH Photography)

In Tudor times, the Red Kite was classed as vermin and people were paid for each bird killed. Persecution continued through the following centuries, until it became extinct in England (1871) and in Scotland (1879).

In 1989 a plan to bring the Red Kite back to England and Scotland was set up by the R.S.P.B. and the Nature Conservancy Council (now Natural England and Scottish Natural Heritage). Between 1995 and 1998 a total of 70 chicks were successfully reintroduced at special protected sites, including one at Fineshade Wood (Northamptonshire). Since then numbers have increased yearly, with approx 100 pairs and 200 chicks in 2009.

Although this has been a great success for the project, the bird is still under threat from being hit by vehicles, electrocution on power lines, shooting, egg collecting and poisoning.

We therefore hope the success will continue, and future generations will be able to see this bird circling the skies of Northamptonshire for many more years.

BIRDS

IT IS THE BIRD'S FEATHERS THAT MAKE IT UNIQUE
IN THE NATURAL WORLD.

Feathers probably evolved from scales but we are unable to say how long it took to complete the change.

The mastery of the air is the main reason why birds have been one of nature's most spectacular successes.

In Northamptonshire we are lucky to be on the migrating paths of many birds, and we also have large numbers of woods and reserves where one can observe both the resident and those that migrate from lands far away.

The following selection of birds covers a very small group of both the garden residents and those that visit our county throughout the year.

KEYS

♂ Male   ♀ Female

BARNACLE GEESE

(Branta leucopsis)
HABITAT – GREGARIOUS ON GRASSLAND AND SALT MARSHES
RARE OCT – MARCH
(RECORDED AT SYWELL COUNTRY PARK 9TH DEC 1999)

BARN OWL

(Tyto alba)
HABITAT – OPEN
WOODLAND, FARMLAND
AND HEATHS.
WIDESPREAD – ALL YEAR.

BLACKBIRD

(Turdus merula)
HABITAT – WOODLAND AND
URBAN AREAS.
WIDESPREAD – ALL YEAR.

BLUE TIT
(Parus caeruleus)
HABITAT – WOODLANDS, URBAN GARDENS, FARMLAND AND MARSHLAND IN WINTER. WIDESPREAD, OFTEN NUMEROUS – ALL YEAR.

BLACKCAP
(Sylvia atricapilla)
HABITAT – PARKS, GARDENS AND WOODLAND
LOCALLY COMMON IN WINTER APRIL – SEPT.

BLACK-HEADED GULL
(Larus ridibundus)
HABITAT – BREEDS COLONIALLY ON FRESH AND SALT MARSHES AND DUNES.
COMMON – OFTEN ABUNDANT – ALL YEAR.

BULLFINCH
(Pyrrhula pyrrhula)
HABITAT – DECIDUOUS AND
OTHER WOODLAND,
SCRUB, PARKS AND
GARDENS.
WIDESPREAD – RARELY
NUMEROUS – ALL YEAR.

CANADA GOOSE
(Branta canadensis)
HABITAT – VAGRANT OF
NORTH AMERICAN
INTRODUCED STOCK,
LARGE FRESH WATER LAKES
AND PARKS.
COMMON – ALL YEAR.

CHAFFINCH
(Fringilla coelebs)
HABITAT – DECIDUOUS,
MIXED CONIFEROUS
WOODLAND, FARMLAND,
PARKS AND GARDENS.
WIDESPREAD, OFTEN
NUMEROUS – ALL YEAR

COMMON BUZZARD
(Buteo buteo)
HABITAT – OPEN
COUNTRYSIDE INCLUDING
FARMLAND AND
MOORLAND.
ALL YEAR.

COAL-TIT
(Parus ater)
HABITAT – WOODLAND OF ALL TYPES,
BUT FAVOURS CONIFERS, GARDENS
AND PARKS. ALL YEAR.

COMMON TERN

(Sterna hirundo)
HABITAT – BREEDS ON
COASTAL BEACHES, INLAND
ON SAND OR GRAVEL PITS,
BESIDE FRESH WATER.
COMMON APRIL – SEPT.

COMMON SNIPE

(Gallinago gallinago)
HABITAT – BREEDS ON FRESH
WATER, MARSHES, SWAMPS,
WET MEADOWS,
MOORLAND.
ALL YEAR.

COCK PHEASENT

(Phasianus colchicus)
HABITAT – FARMLAND,
HEATHS, SCRUB, OPEN
WOODLAND.
WIDESPREAD - ALL YEAR.

COLLARED DOVE
(Streptopella decaocto)
HABITAT – FARMLAND,
PARKS AND URBAN PLACES.
WIDESPREAD - ALL YEAR.

COOT
(Fulica atra)
HABITAT – LARGE EXPANSES
OF FRESH OR BRACKISH
WATER INCLUDING
RESERVOIRS IN WINTER.
COMMON - ALL YEAR.

FIELDFARE
(Turdus pilaris)
HABITAT – BREEDS IN
NORTHERN FORESTS,
PARKS AND GARDENS.
WIDESPREAD.
WINTER VISITOR TO
THE UK.

GADWALL

(Anas strepela)
HABITAT – FRESH WATER
MARSHES AND LAKES.
WIDESPREAD - OCT – APRIL.

GOLDFINCH

(Carduelis carduellis)
HABITAT – OPEN WOODLAND,
HEATH, SCRUB, FARMLAND, PARKS
AND GARDENS.
COMMON – ALL YEAR.

GOLDENEYE

(Bucephala clangula)
HABITAT – BREEDS IN OLD
BURROWS OR HOLLOW TREES
NEAR TO WATER. WINTERS ON
FRESH WATER LAKES.
A REGULAR VISITOR BUT NOT IN
LARGE NUMBERS.
OCT-APRIL.

GREAT SPOTTED WOODPECKER

(Dendrocopos major)
HABITAT – ALL TYPES OF WOODLAND,
URBAN PARKS, GARDENS,
AND FARMLAND WITH LARGE TREES.
WIDESPREAD – OFTEN COMMON
ALL YEAR.

GREAT CRESTED GREBE (SUMMER)

(Podiceaso cristatus)
HABITAT - LARGE REEDS FRINGED
WITH FRESH WATER.
COMMON – ALL YEAR.

GREAT-TIT

(Parus major)
HABITAT – WOODLAND OF
ALL TYPES, FARMLAND,
PARKS AND GARDENS.
COMMON – ALL YEAR.

GREENFINCH

(Carduelis chloris)
HABITAT – OPEN
WOODLAND, SCRUB,
FARMLAND, PARKS AND
GARDENS.
COMMON – ALL YEAR.

GREYLAG GOOSE

(Anser anser)
HABITAT – MOORLAND
AND TUNDRA,
OFTEN CLOSE TO WATER.
WINTERS ON MARSHES,
FARMLAND AND ESTUARIES.
OCT – MAR.

HEDGE
SPARROW/DUNNOCK

(Prunella modularis)
HABITAT – WOODLAND
OF ALL TYPES, FARMLAND,
SCRUB, TOWN PARKS
AND GARDENS.
COMMON – ALL YEAR.

HERON (GREY)
(Ardea cinerea)
HABITAT – WETLANDS OF ALL DESCRIPTIONS
FROM GARDEN PONDS, ESTUARIES WHERE
REED BEDS OR TREES GROW.
COMMON – ALL YEAR.

♂

HOUSE SPARROW
(Passer domesticus)
HABITAT – ASSOCIATED WITH MAN.
FOUND IN TOWNS AND CITIES.
COMMON – ALL YEAR.

♀

LAPWING
(Vanellus vanellus)
HABITAT – BREEDS ON
FIELDS, MOORLAND AND
MARSHES. WINTERS ON
ARABLE GRASSLAND.
COMMON – ALL YEAR.

LITTLE GREBE
(Tachybaptus rufficollis)
HABITAT – SLOW MOVING
RIVERS, CANALS, LAKES AND
RESERVOIRS WITH PLENTY
OF MARGINAL VEGETATION.
COMMON – ALL YEAR.

LITTLE OWL
(Athene noctua)
HABITAT – WOODLAND,
FARMLAND AND HEATHS,
SUBURBAN AREAS.
COMMON – ALL YEAR.

LONG-TAILED TIT

(Aegithalds caudatus)
HABITAT – WOODLAND
UNDERGROWTH, SCRUB,
HEATHLAND AND
FARMLAND HEDGES
COMMON – ALL YEAR.

MAGPIE

(Pica pica)
HABITAT – WOODLAND,
PARKLAND, FARMLAND,
HEATHS AND SCRUB AND
MATURE GARDENS.
COMMON – ALL YEAR.

MALLARD

(Anas plytyrhynchos)
HABITAT – ALMOST ANY
WATERS, FROM SMALL
PONDS TO OPEN SEAS.
COMMON – ALL YEAR.

♂   ♀

MOORHEN

(Gallinula chloropus)
HABITAT – FRESH WATERS
FROM SMALLEST POOLS TO
LARGE LAKES.
COMMON – ALL YEAR.

OYSTERCATCHER

(Haematopus ostralegus)
HABITAT – BREEDS ON COASTAL
MARGINS, GRASSY ISLANDS AND SAND
DUNES. A FEW CAN BE SEEN INLAND
IN THE SUMMER MONTHS.
COMMON – ALL YEAR.

POCHARD

(Aythya ferina)
HABITAT – BREEDS BESIDE
REED-FRINGED FRESH WATERS.
COMMON – ALL YEAR.

PIED WAGTAIL

(Motacilla albayarrelli)
HABITAT – OPENLAND,
GRASS OR FARMLAND,
URBAN PLACES, OFTEN
NEAR WATER.
COMMON – ALL YEAR.

PINTAIL
(Anas acuta)
HABITAT – BREEDS ON
MOORS AND FRESHWATER
MARSHES CLOSE TO WATER.
WINTERS SOMETIMES
ON LAKES.
SEPT – MAR.

REDWING
(Turdus iliacus)
HABITAT – WINTERS IN
WOODLAND AND ON
OPEN FARMLAND
OCCASIONALLY SEEN IN
PARKS AND GARDENS.
WINTER VISITOR
OCT-APRIL.

REED BUNTING
(Emberiza schoenicus)
HABITAT – MARSHY AREAS, WITH DRY SCRUB AND FARMLAND.
COMMON – ALL YEAR.

REED WARBLER

(Acrocephalus scirpaceus)
HABITAT – NORMALLY
REEDBEDS AND SOMETIMES
FRESH WATER MARGINS.
SUMMER VISITOR.

ROBIN

(Erithacus rubecula)
HABITAT – WOODS, PARKS
AND URBAN AREAS.
USUALLY WITH PLENTY OF
UNDERGROWTH COVER.
COMMON – ALL YEAR.

ROOK

(Corvus frugilegus)
HABITAT – ARABLE
FARMLAND WITH ADJACENT
WOODLAND OR PLENTY OF
TALL TREES.
COMMON – ALL YEAR.

SHELLDUCK
(Tadorna tadorna)
HABITAT – ESTUARIES AND
SHELTERED MUDDY COASTS,
OCCASIONALLY ON
FRESH WATER.
ALL YEAR.

SHOVELER
(Anas clypeata)
HABITAT – BREEDS ON
MARSHLAND WITH REED
FRINGED PONDS OR LAKES,
ALSO ON RESERVOIRS.
COMMON – ALL YEAR.

SNOW GOOSE
(Anser caerulescens
hyperboreus)
HABITAT – BREEDS
COLONIALLY ON THE
TUNDRA, NORMALLY CLOSE
TO WATER. VERY RARE.
THIS BIRD WAS SEEN AT
SUMMER LEYS. IT IS POSSIBLE
THAT THE BIRD WAS FROM A
CAPTIVE ESCAPE.

SPARROWHAWK
(Accipiter nisus)
HABITAT – FOREST AND
WOODLAND OF ALL TYPES.
COMMON – ALL YEAR.

STARLING
(Sturnus vulgaris)
HABITAT – ABUNDANT
IN NEARLY ALL TYPES
OF HABITAT.
COMMON – ALL YEAR.

SWALLOW
(Hirundo rustica)
HABITAT – BREEDS IN
BUILDINGS ON FARMLAND
AND URBAN AREAS.
FEEDS ON THE WING
OVER MOST HABITATS.
COMMON - APRIL – OCT.

SWAN (MUTE)
(Cygnus olor)
HABITAT – ALL TYPES OF FRESH WATER,
TOWN PARK LAKES AND LARGE PONDS.
COMMON – ALL YEAR.

TAWNY OWL
(Aythya fuligula)
HABITAT – WOODLAND,
FARMLAND AND URBAN PLACES.
COMMON – ALL YEAR.

TEAL
(Anas crecca)
HABITAT – BREEDS ON
BOGGY OR MARSHY LAND
WITH REED FRINGED POOLS.
WINTERS IN SIMILAR
HABITATS OFTEN WELL
INLAND.
COMMON – OCT – APRIL.

TUFTED DUCK (SUMMER)

(Aythya fuligula)
HABITAT – BREEDS BESIDE
REED-FRINGED PONDS,
DITCHES AND LAKES.
COMMON – ALL YEAR.

TREE SPARROW

(Passer montanus)
HABITAT – WOODLAND,
FARMLAND AND SCRUB. HAS
BECOME UNCOMMON.
'SUMMER LEYS' HAS THE
ONLY LARGE COLONY IN
THE COUNTY.
RARE – ALLL YEAR.

WATER RAIL

(Rallus aquaticus)
HABITAT – REEDBEDS,
OVERGROWN PONDS OR
DITCHES. A VERY SHY BIRD.
COMMON – ALL YEAR.

WREN
(Troglodytes troglodytes)
HABITAT – WELL VEGETATED
AREAS OF ALL KINDS,
ALSO CLIFFS AND
MOUNTAIN SCREENS.
COMMON – ALL YEAR.

WIGEON
(Anas penelope)
HABITAT – BREEDS ON
MOORLAND AND TUNDRA
CLOSE TO WATER. WINTERS
ON LAKES, ESTUARIES,
MARSHES AND GRASSLAND.
COMMON – OCT - APRIL.

WOOD PIGEON
(Columba palumbus)
HABITAT – BREEDS IN
WOODLAND AND SCRUB
FOUND ON FARMLAND AND
IN URBAN PLACES.
COMMON – ALL YEAR.

FLOWERS

CONSIDER THE LILIES OF THE FIELD, HOW THEY GROW; THEY TOIL NOT, NEITHER DO THEY SPIN: AND YET I SAY UNTO YOU, THAT EVEN SOLOMON IN ALL HIS GLORY WAS NOT ARRAYED LIKE ONE OF THESE.

ST. MATTHEW, 6. VS 28, 29.

To restrict the number of species shown in the book, I have excluded those that are well known and included those species that are frequent where they are found, along with those that are either declining or expanding under climate change.

KEYS

■   - Dominant species covering dense populations.

▦   - Species that are frequent where they are found, but not dominant

▣   - Species that grow as isolated individuals among other species, many being rare geographically.

↑   - For expanding species   ↓   - For declining species.

∗   - Scarce found in less than 100 – 1km Squares.

∗∗   - Endangered, found in less than 15 – 1km Squares.

∗∗∗   - Very rare, found in no more than 3 localities in the UK.

The above keys indicate whether the flowers shown are common, frequent, scarce or rare.

USING NORTHAMPTONSHIRE FLORA GROUP RARE PLANT REGISTER BY GILL GENT & ROB WILSON (2008).

●   - Species which are or are becoming rare to find in the county.

RDB. - Red Data Book (2005).

RDB. EN. - Endangered.

RDB.VU. - Vulnerable.

RDB.NT. - Near threatened.

VC32. - Vice-County 32 Northamptonshire.

VC32.3. - Present in 3 sites or less in VC32.

VC32.10. - Present in 10 sites or less in VC32 and in decline.

ABRAHAM, ISAAC AND JACOB
(Trachystemon orientalis)
NATURALISED IN DAMP WOODS AND
WAYSIDES THROUGHOUT THE COUNTY.
MARCH – MAY.

CLOSE UP

● BISTORT
(Persicaria bistorta)
FOUND IN DAMP GRASSLAND, OPEN WOODS, OFTEN NEAR WATER.
■ MAY – AUG. VC 32.3.

BLUE-EYED MARY
(Omphalodes verna)
UNCOMMON ESCAPE BUT
ESTABLISHED IN SOME
WOODS IN THE COUNTY.
▦ MAR – MAY.

CLOSE UP

● BOGBEAN
(Menyanthes trifoliata)
FOUND IN MARSHES, SWAMPS,
FENS AND BOGS.
▦ MAY – JUNE.
VC32.10.

CLOSE UP

BROAD-LEAVED EVERLASTING PEA
(Lathyrus latifolius)
OFTEN FOUND ON RAILWAY BANKS, DITCHES
AND OTHER WASTE GROUND.
⊞ ↑ JUNE – AUG.

CARLINE THISTLE
(Carlina vulgaris)
FOUND ON GRASSLAND ON LIME.
⊡ ↓ JULY – SEPT.

● CATMINT
(Nepeta cataria)
BARE GRASSY PLACES, ROADSIDES ON LIME
SOILS.
⊞ ↓ JUNE – SEPT.
RDB. VU. VC32.10.

CHIVES

(Allium schoenoprasum)
FOUND ON ROCKY GROUND,
OCCASIONALLY NATURALISED IN
OTHER PLACES.
▦ JUNE - SEPT.

CLUSTERED BELLFLOWER

(Campanula glomerata)
FOUND ON GRASSLAND ON LIME.
▦ ↓ JUNE – OCT.

COLUMBINE

(Aquilegia vulgaris)
FOUND IN WOODS, FENS AND DAMP
GRASSLAND.
⊡ ↑ MAY – JULY
VC32.10.

COMMON BROOMRAPE
(Orobanche minor)
A PERENNIAL PARASITE ON ROOTS OF PLANTS.
⊡ ↓ JUNE – SEPT.
VC32.10.

COMMON-STAR-OF-BETHLEHEM
(Ornithogalum angustifolium)
FOUND IN GRASSY, SCRUBBY AND
WOODED PLACES.
⊡ MAY – JUNE.

CORN-COCKLE
(Agrostemma githago)
ONCE ABUNDANT CORNFIELD WEED THAT IS
NOW EFFECTIVELY EXTINCT, EXCEPT AS A
CASUAL SOWN IN 'WILDFLOWER MIXTURES'.
JUNE – AUG.

CORN-MARIGOLD

CORN-MARIGOLD

(Chrysanthemum segetum)
FOUND IN ARABLE FIELDS, ALSO WAYSIDES,
AND PREFERING ACID SOILS.
▦ ↓↓ JUNE – OCT.
RDB.VU.

CREAMY BUTTERBUR

(Petasites japonicus)
FOUND ON WET GROUND BY
STREAMS AND DITCHES, ROAD
VERGES AND DAMP COPSES.
■ ↑ MARCH – MAY.

● DWARF ELDER

(Sambucus ebulus)
NOT NATIVE, NOW USUALLY ONLY
FOUND BY ROADSIDES.
▦ JULY – OCT.
VC32.10.

EYEBRIGHT
(Euphrasia)
EYEBRIGHTS ARE EXTREMELY VARIABLE
IN THEIR TYPE OF FLOWER PATTERNS.
FOUND MAINLY IN GRASSY AND
HEATHY PLACES.
⊡ JUNE – OCT.
VC32.3.

FIGWORT (YELLOW)
(Scrophularia vernalis)
FOUND IN SHADY PLACES OFTEN
AS A GARDEN ESCAPE.
⊡ ↑ APRIL – JUNE.

FORKING LARKSPUR

(Consolida ajacis)
A CORNFIELD WEED NOW NOT SEEN
IN OUR COUNTY ALL THAT OFTEN.
⊡ MAY – SEPT.

FOX-AND-CUBS

(Pilosella aurantiaca)
OFTEN SEEN ALONG RAILWAY
BANKS, CHURCH-YARDS AND
WASTE GROUND.
▦ JUNE – SEPT.

● FRINGED WATER-LILY

(Nymphodides peltatum)
FOUND AT PONDS AND
SLOW FLOWING STREAMS.
⊡ ↑ JUNE – AUG.

● GREATER DODDER
(Cuscuta europaea)
SEEN AROUND ITS FAVOURITE HOST,
NETTLES, ALONG BY RIVERS, CANALS
AND OTHER FRESH WATER.
⊡ ↓ JULY – SEPT.

HARESFOOT CLOVER
(Trifolium arvense)
FOUND IN DRY GRASSY, OFTEN
BARE OR SANDY PLACES.
⊡ ↓ JUNE – AUG.

● HENBANE
(Hyoscyamus niger)
FOUND ON BARE OR DISTURBED GROUND.
⊡ ↓↓ JUNE – AUG.
(Poisonous)
RDB.VU. VC32.10.

HERB PARIS
(Paris quadriflolia)
FOUND IN WOODS, USUALLY ON LIME.
▦ ↓ MAY – JUNE

HOUNDSTONGUE
(Cynoglossum officinale)
FOUND ON DRY, RATHER BARE,
GRASSY PLACES, DUNES AND SHINGLE.
⊡ ↓ MAY – AUG.

JACOB'S LADDER
(Polemonium caeruleum)
FOUND ON GRASSY AND STONY PLACES.
⊡ JUNE – AUG.

JEWEL-WEED
(Impatiens capensis)
FOUND ALONG BY RIVERS AND STREAM SIDES.
■ JULY – SEPT.

KNAPWEED BROOMRAPE
(Orobanche elatior)
FOUND IN GRASSY PLACES MAINLY ON
CHALK AND LIMESTONE.
⊡ JUNE – JULY.

● KNOTTED CLOVER
(Trifolium striatum)
FOUND IN SHORT TURF AND BARE PLACES
OFTEN ON SAND.
⊡ JUNE – JULY.
VC32.10.

KNOTTED HEDGE-PARSLEY

(Torilis nodosa)
FOUND ON ARABLE FIELDS INLAND,
DRY SUNNY BANKS NEAR THE SEA.
⊙ ↓ MAY – JULY.

LARKSPUR

(Consolida ajacis)
A GARDEN ANNUAL AND
CORNFIELD WEED.
⊙ MAY – SEPT.

LILLY-OF-THE-VALLEY

(Connallaria majalis)
FOUND IN DRY WOODS ON
LIMESTONE OR SAND.
▦ ↓ MAY - JUNE.
VC32.10.

LODDON LILLY

(Leucojum aestivum)
FOUND IN WET MEADOWS AND COPSES.
▦ ↑ APRIL – MAY.

● MEADOW SAFFRON

(Colchicum autumnale)
SOMETIMES FOUND IN WOODS
AND DAMP MEADOWS.
⊡ AUG – SEPT.
VERY RARE.

● MONKSHOOD ✻

(Aconitumna pellus)
FOUND IN SHADY STREAM SIDES.
⊡ MAY – SEPT.
(Poisonous Plant)

MOTH MULLEIN

(Verbascum blattaria)
FOUND IN DRY GRASSY AND
BARE WASTE AREAS.
⊡ JUNE – SEPT.

MOTHERWORT

(Leonurus cardiaca)
FOUND IN HEDGE-BANKS, WAYSIDES,
ROUGH OR WASTE GROUND.
⊡ JUNE – SEPT.

● NAVELWORT

(Umbilicus rupestris)
FOUND IN ROCKS, WALLS AND
HEDGE-BANKS.
▦ MAY - AUG.
VC32.10.

ORANGE MULLEIN
(Verbascum phlomides)
FOUND IN DRY GRASSY PLACES AND
BARE WASTE GROUND.
▦ JUNE – AUG.

● PASQUE FLOWER ✳
(Pulsatilla vulgaris)
FOUND IN SHORT TURF USUALLY ON
LIMESTONE.
⊡ ↓ APRIL - MAY.
RDB.VU. VC32.3.

● PENNY ROYAL ✳
(Mentha pulegium)
FOUND ON DAMP HEATHS AND GRASSLAND.
⊡ ↓ AUG – OCT.
RDB. EN. VC32.10

● **PURPLE MILK VETCH**
(Astragalus danicus)
FOUND ON CHALK AND
LIMESTONE TURF.
⊡ ↑ MAY – JULY.
RDB.EN. VC32.10.

● **PURPLE TOADFLAX**
(Linaria purpurea)
FOUND ON WALLS AND
OTHER DRY PLACES.
⊡ ↑ JUNE – AUG.

SAINFOIN
(Onobrychis viciifolia)
FOUND IN DRY GRASSY PLACES
ESPECIALLY ON LIME.
⊡ JUNE - AUG.

SPIKED STAR OF BETHLEHEM ✳
(Ornithogalum pyrenaicum)
FOUND IN GRASSY, SCRUBBY AND
WOODED AREAS. ▦ ↓ JUNE

● SPRING SNOWFLAKE ✳✳✳
(Leucojum vernum)
FOUND IN MOIST SHADY PLACES,
NOW VERY RARE.
⊡ FEB – MARCH.

● STINKING HELLEBORE
(Helleborus foetidus)
FOUND IN THE WILD IN WOODS AND SCRUB.
OFTEN GROWN IN GARDENS.
☉ ↓ FEB – ARPIL.

STRAWBERRY BLITE
(Chenopodium capitatum)
FOUND ON CULTIVATED AND
WASTE LAND, RUBBISH TIPS.
☉ JULY – AUG.

SULPHUR CLOVER
(Trifolium orchroleucon)
FOUND ON GRASSLAND, ROADSIDE VERGES
ESPECIALLY ON CLAY. VERY RARE FOR THE
COUNTY.
☉ ↓ JUNE – JULY.
RDB.NT. VC32.3.

● **TOOTHWORT**
(Lathraea squamaria)
FOUND IN CLUMPS FEEDING ON
THE ROOTS OF HAZEL.
⊡ APRIL – MAY.
VC32.10.

VIPERS BUGLOSS
(Echium vulgare)
FOUND ON DRY, BARE OR SPARSELY
GRASSY PLACES.
▦ ↓ JUNE – SEPT.

● **WILD PANSY**
(Viola tricolor)
FOUND ON BARE
CULTIVATED LAND,
PREFERING SLIGHTLY
ACID SOILS.
▦ ↓ APRIL - SEPT.

WILD TULIP

(Tulipa sylvestris)

FOR A LONG TIME, IT HAS BEEN NATURALIZED IN WOODS AND COPSES.

◉ APRIL – MAY.

UNCOMMON.

YELLOW ARCHANGEL

(Lamiastrum galeobolom)

FOUND IN WOODS, SCRUB AND HEDGE-BANKS.

▦ ↑ APRIL – JUNE.

YELLOW (FRENCH) BARTSIA

(Odontites jauls eotiana)

FOUND ON DAMP, GRASSY PLACES AND WASTE SCRUBLAND. VERY RARE, FOUND ONLY IN ONE AREA OF THE COUNTY. FIRST RECORDED IN 2005.

◉ JUNE – SEPT.

● YELLOW BIRDSNEST

(Monotropa hypopitys)

FOUND IN LEAF LITTER IN BEECH, PINE AND OTHER WOODS.

▦ JULY – AUG.

RDB.EN. VC32.3.

● YELLOW-STAR-OF-BETHLEHEM

(Gagea lutea)

FOUND IN DAMP WOODS.

⊡ FEB - MAR.

VC32.10.

ORCHIDS

**THESE ARE VERY SPECIAL FLOWERS THAT NEED SPECIAL SITES
IN WHICH TO GROW, BUT SADLY HAVE BEEN IN DECLINE THROUGHOUT
THE UK FROM THE TIME OF THE SECOND WORLD WAR.**

They are unbranced Perennials, virtually hairless except for the Helleborines,
flowers being diverse in their shapes, but always two-lipped. The following are
the ones that can still be seen at suitable sites within the county.

BEE ORCHID
(Ophrys apifera)
FOUND ON GRASSLAND AND BARE SOILS.
▦ JUNE - JULY.

● BIRDSNEST ORCHID
(Neottia nidus-avis)
FOUND IN WOODS, ESPECIALLY BEECH IN DEEP SHADE.
⊡ ↓ JUNE – JULY.
RDB-NT. VC32.10.

BROAD LEAVED HELLEBORINE
(Epipactis helleborine)
FOUND MAINLY IN BEECHWOODS.
⊞ MAY – JULY.

BURNT-TIP ORCHID *
(Orchis ustulata)
FOUND ON SHORT TURF ON MAINLY LIME. NOW VERY RARE.
⊡ ↓↓ MAY – JUNE.

COMMON SPOTTED ORCHID

(Dactylorhiza fuchsi)
FOUND IN NUMBER OF HABITATS INCLUDING
GRASSLAND, OPEN WOODS AND FENS.
■ MAY – EARLY AUG.

COMMON TWAYBLADE

(Listera ovata)
FOUND IN WOODS AND GRASSY PLACES.
■ MAY – JULY.

● EARLY MARSH

(Dactylorhiza incarnata)
FOUND IN MARSHES, WET MEADOWS, FENS
AND BOGS.
▦↓ MAY – JULY.
VC32.10.

EARLY PURPLE ORCHID
(Orchis muscula)
FOUND ON GRASSLAND,
WOODS, HEDGE-BANKS.
▦ ↓ APRIL - JUNE.

● FLY ORCHID
(Ophrysinsectifera)
FOUND IN WOODLAND, SCRUB,
GRASSY PLACES AND FENS.
⊡ ↓↓ MAY – JUNE.
RDB-VU. VC32.10.

● FRAGRANT ORCHID

(Gymnadenia Conopsea)
FOUND IN GRASSLAND AND FENS.
■ JUNE – JULY.

● FROG ORCHID

(Dactylorhiza Viridis)
FOUND IN SHORT TURF
AND GRASSY PLACES.
 ↓↓ JUNE – AUG.

● GREATER BUTTERFLY ORCHID

(Platanthera Chlorantha)
FOUND IN WOODS AND GRASSLAND.
 ↓↓ JUNE – JULY.

● **GREEN WINGED ORCHID**
(Anacamptis morio)
FOUND ON GRASSLAND, ESPECIALLY
MEADOWS.
⊡ ↓ MAY – JUNE.

● **HEATH SPOTTED ORCHID**
(Dactylorhiza maculata)
FOUND IN GRASSLAND, OPEN WOODS
AND FENS.
■ MAY – EARLY AUG.

● **MAN ORCHID** ✳
(Orchis anthropophorum)
FOUND IN SHORT TURF ON LIME.
⊡ ↓ MAY – EARLY JULY.

MARSH HELLEBORINE
(Epipactis palustris)
USED TO BE FOUND ON MARSHES,
FENS AND DUNE SLACKS.
NOW VERY RARE FOR THE COUNTY.
■ JULY – AUG.

PYRAMIDAL ORCHID
(Anacamptis pyramidalis)
FOUND IN GRASSLAND,
USUALLY ON LIME.
■ JUNE – EARLY AUG.

● SOUTHERN MARSH ORCHID
(Dactylorhiza praetermissa)
FOUND IN WET MEADOWS,
MARSHES, FENS AND BOGS.
■ MAY – JULY.

VIOLET HELLEBORINE
(Epipactis purpurata)
FOUND IN WOODS OFTEN IN DEEP SHADE.
▣ JULY – SEPT.

FUNGI

MUSHROOMS AND TOADSTOOLS ARE THE REPRODUCTIVE STRUCTURES OF CERTAIN FUNGI. SCIENTIFICALLY, THERE IS NO DIFFERENCE BETWEEN MUSHROOM AND TOADSTOOL, BUT IT HAS BECOME COMMON PRACTICE TO RESTRICT THE TERM MUSHROOM TO THOSE EDIBLE SPECIES.

Fungi lack Chlorophyll and obtain their nutrition by living in or on organic matter of other organisms. The Latin name which is internationally recognised worldwide uses italics. I have included the Latin name and where there is an English name this is also shown. To keep the number of species shown down, I have only included those that the reader should be able to find somewhere within the county.

Agaricus langei
FOUND ON SOILS IN CONIFEROUS OR MIXED WOODS.
OCCURRENCE – EARLY SUMMER TO EARLY AUTUMN.
(INFREQUENT).

Aleuria aurantia
(Orange Peel)
FOUND ON BARE SOIL OR AMONGST GRASS IN LAWNS OR ROADSIDES.
OCCURENCE – EARLY AUTUMN TO EARLY WINTER
(COMMON).

Amanita muscaria
(Fly Agaric)
FOUND ON POOR AND SHADY SOILS,
FAVOURING BIRCH WOODS.
OCCURRENCE – LATE SUMER TO LATE
AUTUMN.
(COMMON).
POISONOUS.

Agaricus silvaticus
FOUND IN GROUPS ON SOIL IN
CONIFEROUS WOODS,
FAVOURING SPRUCE.
OCCURRENCE – LATE SUMMER
TO AUTUMN.
(FREQUENT).

Auricularia, auricula - judae
(Jew's Ear)
FOUND THROUGHOUT THE YEAR, BUT
FRUITING MAINLY LATE SUMMER AND
AUTUMN ON DYING BRANCHES AND TRUNKS
OF LIVING BROAD-LEAF TREES.
(COMMON).

Helvella lacunosa
(Black Helvella)
FOUND IN SMALL GROUPS ON SOIL IN BROAD
LEAVED, CONIFEROUS AND MIXED WOODS.
OCCURRENCE – AUTUMN.
(INFREQUENT).

Boletus edulis
FOUND AS SOLITARY OR SMALL GROUPS
ON SOIL UNDER BROAD-LEAVED OR
CONIFEROUS TREES.
OCCURRENCE – SUMMER TO AUTUMN .
(COMMON).

Clavariadelphus pistillaris
(Giant Club)
FOUND AS SOLITARY OR SMALL GROUPS ON
CALCAREOUS SOIL IN BEECH.
OCCURRENCE – LATE SUMMER TO AUTUMN.
(INFREQUENT).

Clavulina cinerea
(Grey Coral)
FOUND IN SMALL GROUPS
ON SOIL IN WOODS, OFTEN
NEAR TO PATHS.
OCCURRENCE – SUMMER
TO AUTUMN.
(COMMON).

Calocera viscosa
FOUND ON STUMPS
AND ROOTS OF
CONIFEROUS TREES.
OCCURRENCE – AUTUMN.
(COMMON).

Chlorociboria aeruginascens
FOUND IN SMALL GROUPS
ON ROTTING WOOD,
FAVOURING OAK.
OCCURRENCE – LATE
SUMMER TO WINTER.
(COMMON).

Clavulina cristata
(White Coral)
FOUND ON ROTTING
WOOD IN CONIFEROUS
WOODLANDS.
OCCURRENCE – SUMMER
TO LATE AUTUMN.
(COMMON).

Clavulinopsis corniculata
FOUND IN SHORT GRASS OR
TURF SOMETIMES IN OPEN
GRASSY WOODS.
OCCURRENCE – EARLY
SUMMER TO AUTUMN.
(INFREQUENT).

Clitopilus prunulus
(The Miller)
FOUND IN GROUPS ON
SOIL AMONGST GRASS NEXT
TO TREES.
OCCURRENCE – LATE
SUMMER TO AUTUMN.
(FREQUENT).

Clitocybe odora
(Aniseed Toadstool)
FOUND IN SMALL GROUPS ON SOIL IN BROAD-LEAVED WOODS, FAVOURING BEECH. OCCURRENCE – SUMMER TO AUTUMN. (INFREQUENT).

Daedaliopsis confragosa
(Blushing Bracket)
FOUND SINGLY OR IN TIERS, ON DEAD WOOD OF BROAD-LEAF TREES FAVOURING WILLOW, BIRCH AND BEECH. OCCURRENCE – THROUGHOUT THE YEAR. (FREQUENT).

Daldinia concentrica
FOUND ENCRUSTING DEAD WOOD, FAVOURING BEECH AND ASH. OCCURRENCE – THROUGHOUT THE YEAR. (COMMON).

Flammulina velutipes
(Velvet Shank)
FOUND IN TUFTS ON
TRUNKS, STUMPS AND
BRANCHES OF DEAD AND
DISEASED BROAD LEAF TREES.
OCCURRENCE – AUTUMN
TO WINTER.
(COMMON).

Geastrum triplex
(Earthstars)
FOUND IN SMALL GROUPS
ON SOIL AMONGST LEAF
LITTER IN BROAD-LEAVED
WOODS.
OCCURRENCE – LATE
SUMMER TO AUTUMN.
(INFREQUENT).

Gymnopilus junonius
FOUND SOLITARY,
CLUSTERED, CLOSE BY
STUMPS AND OTHER WOOD
OF BROAD-LEAF TREES.
OCCURRENCE – LATE
SUMMER TO AUTUMN.
(FREQUENT).

Helvella crispa
FOUND SOLITARY OR IN SMALL GROUPS ON SOIL IN BROAD-LEAF AND MIXED WOODS.
OCCURRENCE – SUMMER TO AUTUMN.
(FREQUENT).

Helvella ephippium
FOUND SOLITARY OR IN SMALL GROUPS, ON SOIL IN MIXED WOODS.
OCCURRENCE – EARLY SUMMER TO AUTUMN.
(RARE).

Hypoxylon fragiforme
FOUND IN CLUSTERS ON LOGS AND DEAD BRANCHES OF BEECH.
OCCURRENCE – THROUGHOUT THE YEAR.
(COMMON).

Ischnoderma resinosum

A BRACKET FOUND SINGLE
OR IN SMALL TIERS, ON DEAD
WOOD OF BROAD-LEAF
TREES, FAVOURING BEECH.
OCCURRENCE – LATE
SUMMER TO WINTER.
(RARE).

Laccaria amethystea

(The Amethyst Deceiver)
FOUND IN GROUPS ON
SOIL IN CONIFEROUS AND
BROAD-LEAF WOODS,
FAVOURING BEECH.
OCCURRENCE – EARLY
SUMMER TO WINTER.
(VERY COMMON).

Langermannia gigantea

(Giant Puff-Ball)
FRUITING BODY CAN BE UP
TO 80CM ACROSS.
FOUND IN GARDENS,
PASTURE AND SOME WOODS.
OCCURRENCE – SUMMER
TO AUTUMN.
(UNCOMMON).

Lepiota rhacodes
(Shaggy Parasol)
FOUND IN WOODS AND SHUBBERIES OF ALL KINDS, OFTEN WHERE CONIFERS GROW.
OCCURRENCE – SUMMER TO LATE AUTUMN.
(FREQUENT).

Leotia lubrica
(Jelly Babies)
FOUND IN SMALL GROUPS, OFTEN TUFTED IN SOIL OF DAMP WOODS AND UNDER VEGETATION.
OCCURRENCE – LATE SUMMER TO AUTUMN.
(INFREQUENT).

Meripilus giganteus
FOUND AT BASE OF BROAD-LEAF TREES AND STUMPS, FAVOURING BEECH BUT ALSO WITH OAK.
OCCURRENCE – SUMMER TO LATE AUTUMN.
(FREQUENT).

Morchella esculenta

FOUND USUALLY SOLITARY ON SOIL,
IN SCRUB OR OPEN WOODLAND.
OCCURRENCE – SPRING (INFREQUENT).

Mutinus caninus

(Dog Stink-Horn)
FOUND IN SMALL GROUPS ON SOIL
AMONGST LEAF LITTER IN MIXED
WOODS.
OCCURRENCE – SUMMER TO
AUTUMN.
(INFREQUENT).

Morchella elata

FOUND SOLITARY ON SOIL, OFTEN AMONGST
SHORT GRASS, NEAR OR CLOSE TO
CONIFEROUS WOODS.
OCCURRENCE – SPRING
(RARE)

Mucilago crustacea
(Slime Mould)
FOUND SPREADING OVER GRASSES AND OTHER PLANTS AS WELL AS DEAD LEAVES. OCCURRENCE – THROUGHOUT THE YEAR. (FREQUENT).

Neobulgaria pura
FOUND IN GROUPS ON DEAD WOOD OF BROAD-LEAF TREES, FAVOURING BEECH. OCCURRENCE – SUMMER TO AUTUMN. (INFREQUENT).

Otidea onotica
(Hare's Ear)
FOUND IN SMALL GROUPS IN SOIL IN BROAD-LEAF AND MIXED WOODS. FAVOURING BEECH. OCCURRENCE – SPRING TO EARLY AUTUMN. (INFREQUENT).

Oudemansiella mucida
(Porcelain Fungus)
FOUND ON TRUNKS AND
BRANCHES OF BEECH
OFTEN HIGH UP.
OCCURRENCE – SUMMER
TO WINTER.
(COMMON).

Phlebia radiata
FOUND ON THE BARK
OF DEAD DECIDUOUS
TREES, ESPECIALLY BEECH.
OCCURRENCE –
ALL YEAR ROUND.
(COMMON).

Pholiota squarosa
(Shaggy Pholiota)
FOUND IN DENSE, OFTEN
STRIKING GROUPS IN TURF
AT THE BASE OF LIVING
BROAD-LEAF, AND
SOMETIMES CONIFEROUS
TREES.
OCCURRENCE – LATE
SUMMER TO AUTUMN.
(INFREQUENT).

Peziza micropus
FOUND AS SMALL BROWN SAUCER IN SMALL GROUPS. SOME FUSED ON ROTTING WOOD, FAVOURING BEECH. OCCURRENCE – SUMMER TO AUTUMN. (INFREQUENT).

Peziza repanda
FOUND IN SMALL GROUPS ON SOIL AROUND STUMPS AND ON ROTTING SAWDUST AND WOOD. OCCURRENCE – LATE SPRING TO LATE AUTUMN. (INFREQUENT).

Pseudocraterellus undulates
FOUND AS SMALL GREYISH BROWN, TRUMPET-SHAPED AND WRINKLED CAP WITH STEM, IN GROUPS ON SOIL. AMONGST LEAF LITTER IN BROAD-LEAF WOODS. OCCURRENCE – LATE SUMMER TO AUTUMN. (RARE).

Pleurotus ostreatus

(Oyster Mushroom)
FOUND ON TRUNKS AND FELLED TIMBER OF
BROAD-LEAF TREES, FAVOURING BEECH.
OCCURRENCE – THROUGHOUT THE YEAR.
(COMMON).

Ramaria aurea
FOUND ON THE GROUND
IN MIXED WOODS.
OCCURRENCE – AUTUMN.
(RARE).

Ramaria stricta
FOUND ON WOODY DEBRIS IN BROAD-LEAF
WOODS FAVOURING BEECH, SOMETIMES ON
ROTTING CONIFER STUMPS.
OCCURRENCE – SUMMER TO AUTUMN.
(FREQUENT).

Rhodotus palmatus
FOUND IN SMALL GROUPS ON STUMPS, TRUNKS AND FELLED TIMBER OF ELM.
OCCURRENCE – AUTUMN TO WINTER.
(INFREQUENT).

Russula ochroleuca
FOUND AS SOLITARY OR IN SCATTERED GROUPS ON SOIL UNDER BROAD-LEAF AND CONIFEROUS TREES.
OCCURRENCE – LATE SUMMER TO AUTUMN.
(COMMON).

Scleroderma citrinum
(Common Earthball)
FOUND IN SMALL GROUPS ON BARE SOIL OR AMONGST MOSS ON HEATHS AND IN MIXED WOODS.
OCCURRENCE – LATE SUMMER TO AUTUMN.
(VERY COMMON).

Suillus luteus

(Slippery Jack)
FOUND AS SOLITARY OR IN SMALL GROUPS
ON SOIL WITH CONIFEROUS TREES,
FAVOURING SCOTS PINE.
OCCURRENCE – AUTUMN
(COMMON).

Sparassia crispa

(Cauliflower Fungus)
FOUND AS A PARASITIC AT
BASE OF CONIFERS.
OCCURRENCE – SUMMER
TO AUTUMN.
(INFREQUENT).

Thelephora palmata

FOUND ON THE GROUND
NEAR TO CONIFERS.
OCCURRENCE – LATE
SUMMER TO LATE AUTUMN.
(RARE).

Thelephora terrestris
(Earth Fan)
FOUND ON SOIL, AMONGST
LEAF LITTER AND OTHER
DEBRIS IN BROAD-LEAF AND
CONIFEROUS WOODS.
OCCURRENCE – LATE
SUMMER TO AUTUMN.
(FREQUENT).

Tremella foliacea
FOUND SOLITARY OR IN
SMALL GROUPS ON DEAD
AND ROTTING BRANCHES
AND LOGS OF
BROAD-LEAF TREES.
OCCURRENCE – LATE
SUMMER AND AUTUMN.
(RARE).

Tricholomopsis rutilans
(Plums & Custard)
FOUND IN SMALL GROUPS
ON OR CLOSE TO ROTTING
CONIFER STUMPS.
OCCURRENCE – SUMMER
TO AUTUMN.
(COMMON).

Tricholoma gambosum (St. George's Mushroom)
FOUND IN GRASS ON ROADSIDES AND WOOD EDGES OR IN
PASTURE LAND. OCCURRENCE – FOUND TRADITIONALLY ON
23RD APRIL, ST. GEORGE'S DAY.
(OCCASIONAL)

Xylaria polymorpha (Dead Man's Finger)
FOUND IN SMALL TUFTS FROM STUMPS OF BROAD-LEAF TREES,
FAVOURING BEECH. OCCURRENCE – THROUGHOUT THE YEAR.
(COMMON).

GALLS

A GALL IS AN ABNORMAL GROWTH PRODUCED BY A PLANT OR OTHER HOST UNDER THE INFLUENCE OF ANOTHER ORGANISM.

It involves enlargement or proliferation of the host cells and provides both as a shelter and food for the invading organism.

Galls on trees are the best known, however they can be found in a variety of habitats, including Woodlands, old Meadows, Chalk and Limestone Grasslands, Hedgerows, Heaths and Vacant land.

Anoricus kollari (ON OAK)
THESE GALLS ARE PROBABLY MORE FAMILIAR AS THE HARD BROWN 'MARBLES' LEFT ON THE STEMS OF OAK TREES IN WINTER, EACH GALL CONTAINS A SINGLE LARVA OF THE GALL WASP.
(COMMON).

Aceria fraxinivorus

(ON COMMON ASH)
LEAF BUTT TRANSFORMED INTO AN
IRREGULAR 'CAULIFLOWER' GROWTH,
0.5 – 2CM ACROSS, OFTEN MANY IN A
CLUSTER. CONTAINS MITES.
(COMMON).

Aceria macrotrichus

(ON HORNBEAM)
UNDERSIDE OF VEIN MODIFIED INTO
A WAVY RIDGE, CONTAINS MITES.
(COMMON).

Dasineura ulmaria

(ON MEADOW SWEET)
UPPER SURFACE COVERED WITH SMOOTH
ROUND SWELLINGS, 1 – 2MM ACROSS,
USUALLY ON THE VEINS.
(COMMON).

Diplolepis rosae
(Robin's Pincushion)
(ON ROSE)
COVERED WITH LONG BRANCHED WIRY
HAIRS FORMING A MASS UP TO 60MM DIA,
GREEN AT FIRST THEN RED AND LATER
BROWN AND WOODY.
(COMMON). GALL WASP.

Eriophyes tiliae
(ON LARGE LEAVED LIME)
GALLS ARE USUALLY 8MM
TALL WITH POINTED TIPS.
(COMMON).

Hartigiola annulipes
(ON BEECH)
CYLINDRICAL, GALL FALLS TO
THE GROUND IN AUTUMN,
LEAVING CIRCULAR HOLES IN
THE LEAF, PALE GREEN OR
REDDISH BROWN.
(COMMON).

Liposthens glechomae

(ON GROUND IVY)
GLOBULAR HAIRY SWELLINGS
5-20MM DIA ON THE LEAF
UNDERSIDE, GREEN OR
REDDISH IN SUNLIGHT, SOFT
BECOMING HARD.
CONTAINS A WHITE LARVA
OF A WASP.
(COMMON).

Puccinia phragmitis
(ON DOCK)
LEAVES WITH RED OR PURPLE
BLISTER – LIKE SWELLINGS GALL FUNGI.
(COMMON).

Puccinia poarum
(ON COLTSFOOT)
LEAVES WITH THICKENED AREAS ON
UNDERSIDES. ORANGE-RED IN COLOUR.
A RUST.
(LOCALLY COMMON).

Pontania proxima
(ON CRACK WILLOW)
SAUSAGE OR BEAN SHAPED, PROJECTIONS
ON BOTH SIDES OF THE LEAF,
RED IN COLOUR.
(SAWFLY).
(COMMON).

Psyllopsis fraxini
(ON ASH)
BROADER LOOSE ROLL OR FOLDED,
PALE-COLOURED WITH REDDISH ON
VIOLET MARKINGS, CONTAINS NYMPHS.
(COMMON).

Triphragmium ulmariae
(ON MEADOW SWEET)
LEAVES TWISTED AND DISTORTED WITH
STRIKING SWELLINGS BEARING ORANGE
AECIA FUNGI GALL.
(COMMON).

Urophora cardui

(On Creeping Thistle)
A SWELLING IN THE STEM UP TO 30CM,
GREEN AND FLESHY. LATER HARD AND
WOODY, CONTAINS ONE OR MORE
CHAMBERS EACH WITH A LARVA.
(GALL FLY).
MAY – JUNE.
(LOCALLY COMMON).

Horse chestnut leaf mine

FIRST RECORDED IN NORTHANTS IN
2005 AND IS NOW VERY COMMON
THROUGHOUT THE COUNTY.
IT PRODUCES THE MICRO MOTH.
(366a Cameraria ohridella).

INSECTS

MOST INSECTS BEGIN THEIR LIFE AS AN EGG, AFTER A PERIOD OF TIME THAT CAN RANGE FROM DAYS TO MONTHS.

The egg content hatches into a Caterpillar (also known as Larva), which in turn spends most of it's time eating. When it has absorbed the necessary amount of nutrients, it changes into a Pupa. Inside the Pupa, the insect turns into an organised 'soup' in which the cells rearrange themselves into adults.
This process is known as a complete metamorphosis.

Some insects by-pass the 'Pupa Stage' including Aphids and Dragonflies, which turn directly from an adult-like nymph into the adult insect.

KEYS
LS = Life size on picture shown
♂ Male   ♀ Female
ORDER **COLEOPTERA**: BEETLES

Beetles are the largest group of insects in Britain. They make up a very diverse group, occurring both on land and water.

Many eat crops and can be a serious pest. All Beetles have a tough body with the first pair of wings modified into a pair of hard wing cases, some species can live up to almost 3 years.

ASPARAGUS BEETLE (Crioceris asparagi)
THIS BEETLE EATS LEAVES AND CAN BE A SERIOUS AGRICULTURAL AND HORTICULTURAL PEST.
DORMANT IN WINTER.
LENGTH: 5-7MM 4 X LS

BLACK BURYING BEETLE

(Nicrophorus humator)
A BLACK BEETLE, WITH ORANGE-TIPPED
ANTENNAE, FOUND ALL OVER BRITAIN.
LENGTH: 30MM
2 X LS

CARDINAL BEETLE

(Pyrochroa coccinea)
THIS BRIGHTLY COLOURED
BEETLE IS FOUND ON
VEGETATION AND FLOWERS
ALONG WAYSIDES AND
WOODLANDS IN MAY – JUNE.
IT HAS DISTINCTIVE
TOOTHED ANTENNAE.
LENGTH: 15MM
3 X LS

COCKCHAFER
(Melolontha melolontha)
THE LARVAE ARE WHITE GRUBS WHICH FEED
ON PLANT ROOTS. THE LARVAE NEED TWO
OR THREE YEARS TO MATURE. IT IS FOUND
ALL OVER BRITAIN, MAINLY NOCTURNAL AND
ADULTS APPEAR IN MAY – JUNE.
LENGTH: 25MM
2 X LS

DOR BEETLE
(Geotrupes stercorarius)
A GLOSSY, BLUE-BLACK BEETLE WITH RIDGES
RUNNING FROM FRONT TO BACK ON THE
WING CASES. THE LEGS ARE WIDE WITH
SPINES AND TEETH.
LENGTH: 25MM
APRIL – OCTOBER. 2 X LS

DEVIL'S COACH HORSE
(Staphylinus olens)
IN IRISH MYTHOLOGY THIS
BEETLE IS A SYMBOL OF
CORRUPTION, ABLE TO KILL
SIMPLY ON SIGHT.
A LONG, THIN BEETLE, WHICH
LOOKS AND ACTS LIKE AN
EARWIG. IT IS GREY-BLACK IN
COLOUR, WITH A SHORT
WING CASE. DURING THE DAY
IT RESTS AMONG LEAF LITTER
OR UNDER STONES.
LENGTH: 25MM
2 X LS

GREAT DIVING BEETLE

(Dytiscus marginalis)
THIS IS THE MOST COMMON OF THE BRITISH DIVING BEETLES. THE MALE HAS DISC-LIKE SUCKERS ON THE FRONT LEGS WHICH HE USES TO HOLD THE FEMALE WHILE MATING. THE LONG HIND LEGS ARE USED FOR SWIMMING. THE BEETLE CAN LIVE FOR MORE THAN 2 YEARS EATING AQUATIC INSECTS LIKE TADPOLES AND SMALL FISH.
LENGTH: 35MM
LS

GROUND BEETLE

(Harpalus affinis)
THIS BEETLE CAN BE FOUND IN MOST OPEN SITUATIONS ALL YEAR. IT HAS ANTENNAE AND LEGS OF REDDISH YELLOW.
LENGTH: 9 - 12MM
3 X LS

FUNGI BEETLE

(Endomychus coccineus)
THIS BEETLE LOOKS LIKE A LADYBIRD BUT IS MUCH FLATTER AND HAS MUCH LONGER ANTENNAE. THE LARVAE AND ADULT FEED ON VARIOUS FUNGI ASSOCIATED WITH DECAYING WOOD.
APRIL – JULY
LENGTH: 4 - 6MM
4 X LS

LARVA & PUPA

HARLEQUIN LADYBIRD
(Harmonia axyridis)
THIS LADYBIRD WAS FIRST RECORDED IN THE
COUNTY IN 2006. IT IS NOW WIDELY SEEN
THROUGHOUT THE COUNTY.
4 X LS

LONGHORN BEETLE
(Agapanthia villosoviridescens)
FOUND MAINLY IN DAMP PLACES, LARVAE
DEVELOP IN THE STEMS OF THISTLES AND
VARIOUS OTHER HERBACEOUS PLANTS.
MAY – JULY.
LENGTH: 10 - 25MM
LS

LEAF WEEVIL
(Phyllobius pomaceus)
ABOUT 10MM LONG WITH
A NARROW BODY, GREENISH
OR BLUISH SCALES.
NORMALLY FOUND NEAR
TO WATER.
LENGTH: 7 - 10MM
(COMMON).
4 X LS

LESSER STAG BEETLE
(Dorcus parallelipipedus)
THIS GREY-BLACK BEETLE IS
MORE COMMON THAN THE
STAG BEETLE BUT MUCH
LESS IMPRESSIVE IN
APPEARANCE. NOT SEEN
TOO OFTEN AS THEY ARE
MORE ACTIVE AT NIGHT.
THEY CAN BE FOUND IN OR
ON ROTTING TIMBERS,
ESPECIALLY BEECH,
ELM AND ASH.
LENGTH: 32MM
ALL YEAR. LS

LILY BEETLE
(Lilioceris lilii)
A SMALL RED BEETLE WHICH
MAY BE FOUND IN GARDENS
WHERE LILIES ARE GROWN.
THE LARVAE EAT THE LEAVES
OF THE LILY PLANTS.
LENGTH: 10MM
APRIL – AUGUST.
4 X LS

MAY BEETLE
(Melolontha hippocastani)
THIS BEETLE EATS THE LEAVES OF DECIDUOUS
TREES, FOUND IN HEATHS AND WOODS.
LENGTH: 22 - 26MM
1 1/4X LS
(UNCOMMON)

ROSE CHAFER
(Cetonia aurata)
AN ATTRACTIVE GREEN BEETLE WHICH FLIES
FROM MAY TO AUG. THEY CAN BE FOUND ON
THE PETALS OF LARGE FLOWERS,
PARTICULARLY ROSES, ON WHICH THEY FEED.
LENGTH: 20MM
2 X LS

SEXTON BEETLE
(Nicrophorus vespilloides)
THE BLACK AND ORANGE
BEETLE IS ALSO KNOWN AS
BURYING, OR GRAVE-DIGGING
BEETLE BECAUSE OF ITS
HABITAT OF BURYING DEAD
ANIMALS AS FOOD FOR
ITS' OFFSPRING.
LENGTH: 16MM
2.5 X LS

SOLDIER BEETLE

(Rhagonycha fulva)
THEY ARE A FAMILIAR SIGHT
IN EARLY SUMMER IN
MEADOWS WHERE THEY
COLLECT ON LARGE
FLOWERS, SUCH AS COW
PARSLEY, FEEDING ON SOFT
BODIED INSECTS.
MAY – JULY.
LENGTH: 10MM
4 X LS

TWO-SPOT FLOWER BEETLE

(Malachius bipustulatus)
LESS THAN 10MM LONG
THIS IS A QUITE
CONSPICUOUS BEETLE,
IT HAS A SLENDER BODY,
BRIGHT METALLIC GREEN
EXCEPT FOR 2 LARGE RED
DOTS AT THE REAR.
FOUND IN ROUGH
FLOWERY PLACES.
(COMMON).
LENGTH: 5 - 8MM
APRIL – JULY. 3 X LS

VARIABLE LONGHORN BEETLE

(Stenorus meridianus)
THIS ORANGEY BEETLE CAN
BE SEEN IN MANY PARTS OF
BRITAIN FROM MAY TO JULY.
IT BREEDS IN ROTTING
STUMPS OF SOUR CHERRY,
ASH AND SALLOW.
LENGTH: 20MM
MAY – JULY.
2 X LS

VINE WEEVIL
(Otiorhynchus sulcatus)
THIS WEEVIL IS A
TROUBLESOME GARDEN PEST
WHICH CHEW THE LEAVES
AND SHOOTS OF MANY
PLANTS. THE LARVAE DO
THE MOST DAMAGE BY
DESTROYING ROOTS OF
POT PLANTS AND GREEN
HOUSE CROPS.
LENGTH: 8 - 12MM
3 X LS

VIOLET GROUND BEETLE
(Carabus violaceus)
THE VIOLET GROUND BEETLE NAMED AFTER
THE VIOLET SHEEN ON ITS BACK WING-CASES,
IS ONE OF THE LARGEST SPECIES.
IT IS USEFUL TO FARMERS AND GARDENS AS
IT EATS LARGE NUMBERS OF PLANT
FEEDING INSECTS.
LENGTH: 28MM
ALL YEAR.
LS

WASP BEETLE
(Clytus arietis)
A BLACK BEETLE WITH YELLOW BANDS,
LONG ORANGE LEGS AND LONG ANTENNAE.
IT IS USUALLY SEEN IN WOODLAND IN MAY
AND JUNE, FEEDING ON THE NECTAR OF
VARIOUS FLOWERS, INCLUDING COW PARSLEY
AND BRAMBLES.
LENGTH: 10MM
MAY – AUGUST.
3 X LS

ORDER DERMAPTERA : EARWIGS

THESE INSECTS ARE RECOGNISED BY THE TWEEZER-LIKE PINCERS,
STRONGLY CURVED IN MALE, AND STRAIGHT IN FEMALES.
THERE ARE ONLY FOUR SPECIES NATIVE TO THE UK.

COMMON EARWIG (Forficula avricularia)

A SMALL BEETLE LIKE INSECT WITH PROMINENT PINCERS AT
THE REAR END OF THE BODY, AND SHORT WINGS. MAINLY
ACTIVE AT NIGHT. LENGTH: UP TO 13MM. 3 X LS

ORDER DIPTERA : TRUE FLIES

DIPTERA MEANS TWO-WINGED AND
REFERS TO THOSE INSECTS HAVING JUST
TWO WINGS, ALTHOUGH THERE ARE
SOME WINGLESS SPECIES.

They are liquid-feeders having piercing mouths
which are used for sucking up food material. Fly
larvae are maggots and will eat almost anything
from fungi, rotten wood, decaying flesh and dung.
Many larvae of leaf-miners and others induce
Gall-formation (see pages 84-89).

BEEFLY (Bombylius major)

SEEN FLYING LOW AMONG THE PRIMROSES
IN EARLY SPRING. THE FEMALE SCATTERS
HER EGGS WHILE FLYING. LENGTH: 11MM.
MARCH – JUNE.
2 X LS

COMMON BLUEBOTTLE

(Calliphora s.p.)
THIS IS A LARGE METALLIC-BLUE FLY THAT
BUZZES LOUDLY ON WINDOW PANES.
THEY LAY THEIR EGGS ON EXPOSED MEAT,
TURNING INTO MAGGOTS WHICH
THEN EAT IT.
LENGTH: 11MM
3 X LS

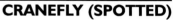

CRANEFLY (SPOTTED)

(Nephrotoma crogata)
FOUND IN MANY HABITATS BUT ESPECIALLY
IN DAMP AREAS.
MAY – AUG.
LENGTH: 15 - 20 MM
1 1/4 X LS

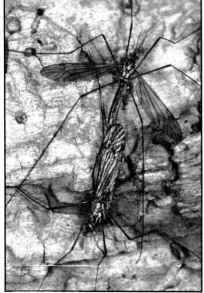

BLACK & YELLOW CRANEFLY

(Nephrotoma maculosa)
THIS BLACK AND YELLOW CRANEFLY IS VERY
COMMON IN FIELDS AND GARDENS, IN THE
AUTUMN EVENINGS.
LENGTH: 18 MM
LS

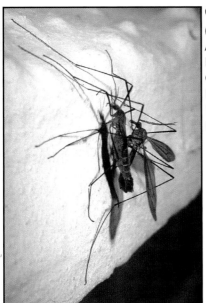

CRANEFLY (DADDY-LONG LEGS)

(Tipula paludosa)
A GREY-BROWN FLY WITH A LONG THIN
BODY AND NARROW WINGS. IT IS THE MOST
COMMON AND WIDESPREAD CRANEFLY
IN THE UK.
LENGTH - 20 MM
MAY – OCTOBER.
LS

DUNGFLY

(Scathophaga spercoraria)
A SLENDER-BODIED FLY WITH GOLDEN-
YELLOW HAIRS, MALES ARE BROWNISH
FEMALES ARE DULLER AND LESS HAIRY.
VERY COMMON.
LENGTH: 8 - 10MM
APRIL – SEPTEMBER.

4 X LS

FLESHFLY

(Sarcophaga carnaria)
A LARGE FLY WITH A CHEQUERED BODY THAT
OCASSIONALLY COMES INDOORS WHEN
FOOD IS LEFT UNCOVERED.
LENGTH: 16MM

2 X LS

HORSEFLY
(Chrysops caecutiens)
THIS COMMON HORSEFLY IS EASILY
RECOGNISED BY ITS RED AND GREEN EYES.
IT WILL BITE HUMANS.
LENGTH: 11MM
MAY – SEPTEMBER.
2 X LS

HOVERFLY
(Episyrphus balteatus)
THIS IS THE MOST FREQUENTLY
SEEN HOVERFLY. THE ORANGE BODY
WITH DOUBLE BLACK STRIPES ACROSS IT
CAN OCCUR IN ALMOST ANY HABITAT
WHERE FLOWERS GROW.
LENGTH: 10 -15 MM
MARCH – NOVEMBER. 2 X LS

HOVERFLY
(Helophilus pendulus)
THIS IS A VERY ATTRACTIVE AND DISTINCTIVE
HOVERFLY. WINGSPAN 25MM. THORAX
STRIPED WITH 3 BLACK STRIPES, LEGS PALE
YELLOW. FOUND IN ROUGH FLOWERY
HABITAT NEAR TO WATER. COMMON
LENGTH: 12MM
APRIL – OCTOBER. 3 X LS

HOVERFLY

(Scaeva pyrastri)
FOUND IN FLOWERY PLACES NEARLY
EVERYWHERE, COMMON IN GARDENS.
LENGTH - 15MM
JUNE – OCTOBER.
LS

HOVERFLY

(Volucella inanis)
A LARGE HOVERFLY WITH THE TYPICAL
VOLUCELLA SHAPE WITH A WING-SPAN
OF OVER 30MM. THE ABDOMEN IS
BRIGHT YELLOW WITH 2 CLEAR BLACK
BANDS, LEGS ORANGE. CAN BE FOUND
IN WOODS, PARKS AND GARDENS.
LENGTH: 15MM
JULY – OCTOBER.
2 X LS
(NOT COMMON - VERY LOCAL).

MOSQUITO LARVAE (COMMON GNAT)

(Culex pipiens)
THIS COMMON GNAT
BREEDS IN PONDS, DITCHES
AND WATER BUTTS.
FLIES AT SUNSET WITH
A BUZZING SOUND.
IT ONLY OCCASIONALLY
BITES HUMANS.
LENGTH: 6MM
5 X LS

NOONFLY

(Mesembrina meridiana)
A MEDIUM-SIZED FLY WITH
ABOUT 10MM DARK BODY
AND REDDISH EYES.
THE MOST CONSPICUOUS
FEATURE IS THE YELLOWISH
BROWN ON THE WINGS.
FOUND IN FLOWERY
PLACES OFTEN SUNBATHING
ON POSTS.
(COMMON)
LENGTH: 12MM
MARCH – OCTOBER.
2 X LS

ST. MARK'S FLY

(Bibio marci)
A LARGE, HEAVILY BUILT
FLY WHICH SITS ON
PLANTS IN SPRING.
LENGTH: 13MM
APRIL – JUNE.
3 X LS

TACHINIDFLY
(Phyrxe vulgaris)
THIS SPECIES WHICH OCCURS
THROUGHOUT THE UK, RESEMBLES
THE HOUSEFLY CLOSELY.
IT CAN BE FOUND NEAR TREES
FROM MAY TO LATE SEPT.
IT'S LARVAE ARE INTERNAL PARASITES
IN CATERPILLARS.
LENGTH: 10MM
3 X LS

TWIN-LOBED DEERFLY (Chrysops relictus)
RARELY FAR FROM WATER AND MOST COMMON IN MARSHY AREAS
BETWEEN MAY – SEPT.
LENGTH: 10 - 12MM
3 X LS

ORDER EPHEMEROPTERA : MAYFLIES
THESE ARE FLIMSY INSECTS WHICH MOSTLY FLY AT NIGHT AND RARELY STRAY FROM WATER.

MAYFLY
(Ephemera vulgata)
ON SUMMER EVENINGS AROUND STREAMS AND LAKES, YOU CAN COME ACROSS BRITAIN'S BIGGEST MAYFLY. IT HAS LARGE FOREWAYS AND SMALL HINDWINGS. WHEN AT REST, IT HOLDS THE WINGS VERTICALLY. IT FLIES MOSTLY AT NIGHT AND RARELY STRAYS FROM WATER.
APRIL – AUGUST.
LS

ORDER HEMIPTERA : BUGS, APHIDS, THRIPS, MIRID/CASPID BUGS

MIRID/CASPID BUGS
THE FOREWINGS OF THESE BUGS IF PRESENT ARE USUALLY FAIRLY SOFT WITH PROMINENT TRIANGULAR AREA IN FRONT OF THE MEMBRANE.

It differs in colour from the rest of the wing. The bug is found in a variety of habitats including parks and gardens. Most Mirids are herbivorous with fruit and seed being their diet.

MIRID BUG
(Liocoris tripustulatus)
JUNE – SEPT.

MIRID BUG

(Rhabdomiris striatellus)

MIRID BUG
(Closterotomus norwegicus)

MIRID BUG
(Miridius quadrivirgatus)
(UNCOMMON FOR THE COUNTY)

FOREST SHIELD BUG
(Pentatoma rufipes)
A LARGE BROWN SHEILD BUG WITH ORANGE
LEGS AND A NOTICEABLE ORANGE OR
YELLOW TIP TO THE TRIANGULAR
SCUTELLUM. FOUND MAINLY IN OAK WOODS,
ALSO IN ORCHARDS & GARDENS.
LENGTH: 11 – 14MM
(COMMON). JUNE – NOVEMBER.
4 X LS

HAWTHORN SHIELD BUG
(Acanthosoma haemorrhoidale)
A LARGE BRIGHTLY COLOURED BUG,
A WOODLAND SPECIES,
ALSO FOUND IN GARDENS AND PARKS.
LENGTH 13 -15MM (COMMON)
ALL YEAR. 2 X LS

SQUASH BUG
(Coreus marginatus)
A LARGE, MOTTLED BROWN BUG WITH A
BROAD ABDOMEN. FOUND IN A WIDE VARIETY
OF HABITATS, INCLUDING HEDGEROWS,
WASTELAND AND DAMP AREAS.
LENGTH 13 – 15MM
(COMMON)
AUGUST – JULY. 2 X LS

SHIELD BUG

(Picromerus bidens)
A BROWN SHIELD BUG WITH LARGE
THORN-LIKE EXTENSIONS TO THE
PRONOTURN. USUALLY FOUND IN
LUSH VEGETATION, AT SHELTERED
SITES BY WATER MARGINS.
LENGTH: 12 – 13.5MM
JULY – NOVEMBER.
3 X LS

SQUASH BUG

(Rhopalus subrufus)
ONE OF 3 VERY SIMILAR BUGS.
CAN BE RECOGNISED BY THE LIGHT
AND DARK BANDING ON THE MARGINS
OF THE ABDOMEN.
FOUND IN WOODLAND CLEARINGS
AND OTHER SCRUBBY PLACES.
LENGTH: 7 - 8MM
ALL YEAR.
4 X LS

BLACK BEAN APHID
(Aphis fabae)
THIS APHID IS DULL BLACK AND UP
TO 3MM LONG. IT IS USUALLY SEEN
FROM LATE MAY IN DENSE CLUSTERS
ON THE UPPER STEMS, SHOOTS
AND YOUNG LEAVES OF THE BROAD
AND RUNNER BEAN PLANT.

BLACK AND RED FROGHOPPER
(Cercopis vulnerata)
THIS IS A STRIKING COLOURED
SPECIES, SEEN IN EARLY SUMMER
CLINGING TO LUSH GRASS AND
LOW VEGETATION.
LENGTH: 10MM
APRIL – AUGUST.
3 X LS

COMMON FROGHOPPER
(Philaenus spumarius)
THE ADULTS CAN BE SEEN ALL OVER BRITAIN
BETWEEN MAY – SEPT. LEAPING FROM STEM TO
STEM ON GRASSES AND OTHER PLANTS. THEIR
LARVAE EXUDE THE FAMILIAR FROTHY
'CUCKOO-SPIT' TO HIDE THEMSELVES FROM
PREDATORS. LENGTH: 8MM.
JUNE – SEPTEMBER. 4 X LS

GREEN FLY

(Macrosiphum rosae)

THESE COMMON GREEN APHIDS INFEST ROSE BUSHES IN SPRING. IN SUMMER, THEY MOVE TO OTHER PLANTS INCLUDING SCABIOUS AND TEASELS.

LENGTH: 5MM

2 X LS

ORDER HYMENOPTERA : BEES, WASPS, ANTS, SAWFLIES, ICHNEUMONS

BEES, WASPS AND ANTS – All these species have the characteristic 'Wasp Waist'. They have a sting used for defence or to paralyse their prey.

SAWFLIES – Most adults feed on Pollen and Nectar, adults are mainly day flying. The eggs are usually laid inside plant tissues, and the larvae are all vegetarians.

ICHNEUMONS – The antennae of these insects consist of at least 16 small segments. They are all Parasitoids attacking the Caterpillars of Butterflies and Moths.

BLACK GARDEN ANT

(Lasius niger)

THE BLACK GARDEN ANTS OCCUR IN GARDENS, GRASSLANDS, HEATHS AND WOODS. THEY MAKE THEIR NESTS UNDER PLANTS, OLD LOGS AND STONES.
IN LATE SUMMER SWARMS OF FLYING ANTS OCCUR WHEN THE QUEENS AND MALES RISE INTO THE AIR IN DENSE CLOUDS TO MATE. THEY FEED ON THE HONEYDEW OF APHIDS, PARTICULARLY THOSE OF THE BLACK BEAN APHID WHICH ATTACKS BROAD AND RUNNER BEANS.
LENGTH: WORKER 5MM. LS

BROWN-BANDED CARDER BEE

(Bombus humilis)
THIS BEE IS NEVER VERY COMMON, BUT CAN BE FOUND IN GRASSLANDS.
LENGTH: 9 – 15MM
2 X LS

BUFF-TAILED BUMBLE BEE

(Bombus terrestris)
THIS BEE IS COMMON IN GARDENS AND MANY OTHER HABITATS.
LENGTH: 10 – 16MM
2 X LS

COMMON WASP

(Vespula vulgaris)
THIS WASP IS MOST FREQUENTLY SEEN IN LATE SUMMER AND AUTUMN WHEN THEY SEEK OUT SWEET FOOD SUCH AS RIPE FRUIT. THE WASPS NEST IS USUALLY BUILT UNDERGROUND IN BURROWS LEFT BY SMALL ANIMALS SUCH AS MICE OR VOLES.
LENGTH: 22MM
2 X LS

DIGGER BEE

(Nomada flava)
THIS SPECIES AN ALMOST
HAIRLESS, WASP-LIKE BEE
THAT LIVES AS A CUCKOO
IN THE NEST OF THE
MINING BEE.
LENGTH: 12MM
APRIL – JULY.
2 X LS

GIANT WOOD WASP

(Urocerus gigas)
A LARGE BLACK AND YELLOW WASP WITH
NO 'WAIST' BETWEEN THE THORAX AND
ABDOMEN. FOUND IN PINE WOODS.
LENGTH: 20 - 30MM
MAY – OCTOBER.
2 X LS

HORNET

(Vespa crabro)
THE LARGEST BRITISH WASP, NOW NOT SO
COMMON. THE WASP USUALLY NESTS IN
HOLLOW TREES. ALTHOUGH IT HAS A
POWERFUL STING, IT TENDS TO BE LESS
AGGRESSIVE THAN OTHER WASPS.
LENGTH: 20 – 30MM
2 X LS

SIDE-VIEW

ICHNEUMON
(Ophion luteus)
COMMON SPECIES WHICH IS
MAINLY NOCTURNAL, CAN BE
SEEN IN ROUGH FLOWERY
HABITATS AND GRASSLANDS.
LENGTH: 15 - 20MM
JUNE – OCTOBER.
2 X LS

ICHNEUMON
(Ichneumon suspiciosus)
A COMMON SPECIES IN A GROUP HAVING BROAD
RED OR ORANGE ABDOMEN BAND AND PALE SPOTS
AT THE REAR. ALL YEAR.
LENGTH: 15 – 18MM
2 X LS

SAWFLY
(Croesus septentrionalis)
THE LARVAE CAN BE FOUND
FEEDING AROUND THE LEAF
EDGES, IF DISTURBED THEY
RAISE THEIR REAR ENDS IN
UNISON AND RELEASE A
PUNGENT ODOUR.
MAY – SEPT.
LENGTH: 9 – 12MM. 1½ X LS

ORDER LEPIDOPTERA : BUTTERFLIES

THE BUTTERFLIES FORM THE ORDER OF LEPIDOPTERA WHICH FORMS THE SECOND LARGEST OF ALL THE INSECT GROUPS.

The main characteristic of the species is in the possession of minute scales, which clothe the wings and body and give the wings their colourful pattern.

The word Lepidoptera literally means 'scale wings' the other major feature of these insects is the slender Proboscis or drinking tube.

All the Butterflies included in this book have been recorded in Northamptonshire including several rare migrants.

KEYS
FP = Food plants of the butterflies larva
CHECK LIST N° = Taken from J. D. Bradley List 2000
LS = Life size on picture shown
♂ Male   ♀ Female

BERGER'S CLOUDED YELLOW (1544)
(Colias australis)
FP HORSESHOE AND COMMON VETCH.
LARVA: JAN – DEC.
(VERY RARE MIGRANT).
RECORED IN IRCHESTER COUNTRY PARK 28TH MAY 1998.
FLIGHT: MAY – SEPT.
2 X LS

BLACK HAIRSTREAK (1559)
(Strymonidia pruni)
FP. BLACKTHORN. LARVA: JUNE – AUG.
THIS IS A RARE SPECIES FOUND IN GLAPTHORN COW
PASTURE IN GOOD NUMBERS.
FLIGHT: JUNE – AUG.
2 X LS

BRIMSTONE (1546)
(Goneptery rhamni)
FP. BUCKTHORN AND ALDER
BUCKTHORN.
LARVA: JUNE – JULY
THE MALE IS A BRIGHTER YELLOW.
FLIGHT: FEB – SEPT.
2 X LS

CAMBERWELL BEAUTY
(1596)
(Nymphalis antiopa)
FP. SALLOW, BIRCH AND
OTHER TREES.
LARVA: APRIL – JULY
THIS IS A VAGRANT SUMMER
VISITOR TO THE UK FROM
TIME TO TIME.
FLIGHT: JUNE – AUG.
LS

CHALKHILL BLUE
(1575)
(Lysandra coridon)
FP. SMALL LEGUMES
ESPECIALLY HORSESHOE
VETCH.
LARVA: APRIL – JUNE
A VAGRANT SPECIES
NORMALLY FOUND ON
CHALKY GRASSLAND.
FLIGHT: JUNE – AUG.
2 X LS

CLOUDED YELLOW
(1545)
(Collas crocea)
FP. CLOVERS, VETCHES.
LARVA: JAN – DEC.
MIGRANT SUMMER VISITOR
TO THE COUNTY.
FLIGHT: APRIL – OCT.
LS

COMMA (1598)
(Polygonia c-album)
FP. STINGING NETTLE
LARVA: MAY – SEPT.
FLIGHT: MARCH – SEPT.
LS

COMMA (SIDEVIEW) 2XLS

COMMON BLUE (1574)
(Polyommatus icarus)
FP. CLOVERS AND
BIRDSFOOT TREFOIL
LARVA: JAN – DEC.
FLIGHT: MAR – OCT.
LS

DARK GREEN FRITILLARY (1607)

(Mesoacidalia aglaja)
F.P. VIOLETS
LARVA: AUG – JUNE.
A VAGRANT VISITOR TO THE
COUNTY, NORMALLY FOUND
ON ROUGH GRASSLAND
SOUTH OF THE COUNTY.
FLIGHT: JUNE - AUG.
LS

DARK GREEN FRITILLARY - SIDE VIEW LS

GATEKEEPER (1625)

(Pyronia tithonus)
F.P. VARIOUS FINE LEAVED
GRASSES.
LARVA: AUG – JUNE.
FLIGHT: JULY – SEPT.
LS

GREEN-VEINED WHITE
(1551)
(Pieris napi)
FP. VARIOUS CRUCIFERS,
GARLIC MUSTARD,
CUCKOO FLOWER.
LARVA: APRIL – OCT.
FLIGHT: MAR – NOV.
LS

GRIZZLED SKIPPER
(1534)
(Pyrgus malvae)
FP. WILD STRAWBERRY
CINQUEFOILS.
LARVA: JUNE – OCT.
FLIGHT: APRIL – AUG.
2 X LS

HOLLY BLUE (1580)
(Celastrina argiolus)
FP. HOLLY (SPRING)
IVY (AUTUMN)
LARVA: MAY – SEPT.
FLIGHT: APRIL – SEPT.
LS

HOLLY BLUE (1580)

(Celastrina argiolus)
FP. HOLLY (SPRING)
IVY (AUTUMN)
LARVA: MAY – SEPT.
FLIGHT: APRIL – SEPT.
LS

GREEN HAIRSTREAK
(1555)
(Callophrys rubi)
FP. GORSE, BROOM,
HEATHER, ROCK ROSE AND
OTHER LOW-GROWING
PLANTS.
LARVA: MAY – AUG.
FLIGHT: MAR – JULY.
2 X LS

LARGE SKIPPER (1531)

(Ochlodes venatus)
FP. COCKSFOOT AND OTHER
COARSE GRASSES.
LARVA: JAN – DEC.
FLIGHT: MAY – SEPT.
1 1/2 X LS

LARGE WHITE (1549)
(Pieris brassicae)
FP. MAINLY CULTIVATED BRASSICAS.
LARVA: MAY – NOV.
FLIGHT: APRIL – OCT.
LS

MARBLED WHITE (1620)
(Melanargia galathea)
FP. RED FESCUE AND OTHER GRASSES.
LARVA: JULY – MAY.
(THIS IS A DECLINING SPECIES
IN THE COUNTY 2010)
FLIGHT: JUNE – JULY.
LS

MARBLED WHITE SIDE VIEW

MEADOW BROWN
(1626)
(Maniola jurtina)
FP. MEADOW GRASSES.
LARVA: JAN – DEC.
FLIGHT: JAN – DEC.
LS

ORANGE-TIP (1553)
(Anthocaris cardamines)
FP. VARIOUS CRUCIFERS,
GARLIC MUSTARD AND
CUCKOO FLOWER.
LARVA: MAY – AUG.
FLIGHT: APRIL – JUNE.
LS

PAINTED LADY (1591)
(Cynthia cardui)
FP. THISTLES, STINGING
NETTLE AND MALLOW.
MIGRANT SPECIES NUMBERS
VARY FROM YEAR TO YEAR
(RECORDED NUMBERS
ARRIVED IN THE UK 2009)
FLIGHT: APRIL – OCT.
LS

PAINTED LADY SIDE VIEW LS

PEACOCK (1597)
(Inachisio)
FP. COMMON STINGING
NETTLE.
LARVA: MAY – JULY
FLIGHT: MARCH – MAY &
JULY – SEPT.
LS

PURPLE HAIRSTREAK (1557)
(Quercusia quercus)
FP. OAK AND OCCASIONALLY ASH.
LARVA: APRIL – JUNE
FLIGHT: JUNE – SEPT.
LS

PURPLE EMPEROR (1585)
(Apatura iris)
FP. SALLOWS
LARVA: AUG – JUNE
FLIGHT: JULY – AUG.
3/4 X LS

RED ADMIRAL (1590)
(Vanessa atalanta)
FP. COMMON STINGING NETTLE.
LARVA: APRIL – OCT.
FLIGHT: MAY – OCT.
LS

RINGLET (1629)
(Aphantopus hyperantus)
FP. MANY TYPES OF GRASSES.
LARVA: AUG – MAY
FLIGHT: JUNE – AUG.
LS

SMALL COPPER (1561)
(Lycaena phlaeas)
FP. COMMON AND SHEEP'S SORREL,
SOMETIMES DOCKS.
LARVA: JAN – DEC.
FLIGHT: FEB – NOV.
1 1/2 X LS

SMALL SKIPPER (1526)
(Thymelicus sylvestris)
FP. VARIOUS GRASSES
ESPECIALLY YORKSHIRE FOG.
LARVA: JAN – DEC.
FLIGHT: MAY – AUG.
2 X LS

SPECKLED WOOD (1614)

(Pararge aegeria)
FP. MANY TYPES OF GRASSES.
LARVA: JAN – DEC.
FLIGHT: MAR – OCT.
1 1/2 X LS

SMALL TORTOISESHELL (1593)

(Aglais urticae)
FP. COMMON AND SMALL
NETTLE.
LARVA: MAY – SEPT.
FLIGHT: MAR – OCT.
LS

SMALL WHITE (1550)

(Piers rapae)
FP. WILD AND CULTIVATED
BRASSICAS.
LARVA: JAN – DEC.
FLIGHT: MAR – OCT.
LS

♀

WALL BROWN (1615)
(Lasiommata megera)
FP. COCKSFOOT, YORKSHIRE
FOG AND OTHER COARSE
GRASS.
LARVA: JAN – DEC.
FLIGHT: MAR – OCT.
(THIS IS A DECLINING SPECIES
2010)
1 1/2 × LS

WHITE ADMIRAL
(1584)
(Limentitis camilla)
FP. HONEYSUCKLE
LARVA: JULY – MAY
FLIGHT: JUNE – AUG.
LS

WHITE ADMIRAL (UNDERSIDE) LS

WHITE LETTER HAIRSTREAK (1558)

(Strymonidia w-album)
FP. ELMS ESPECIALLY WYCH ELM.
LARVA: APRIL – JULY
FLIGHT: JUNE – AUG.
3 X LS

WOOD WHITE (1541)

(Leptidea sinapis)
FP. MEADOW VETCHLING, TUFTED
VETCH.
LARVA: APRIL – SEPT.
FLIGHT: APRIL – SEPT.
4 X LS

ORDER **LEPIDOPTERA** : MOTHS

I HAVE ONLY INCLUDED THE HAWK-MOTHS IN THIS PUBLICATION.

For a more detailed look at Moths found in the County, Refer to my books on Micro and Macro published in (2005, 2006 & 2009).

KEYS
FP = Food plant of larvae
DKT = Indicates moths that can be seen at dusk time.
LS = Life size on picture shown

BEDSTRAW HAWK MOTH (1987)
(Hyles galli)
MAY – AUG.
FP. BEDSTRAWS
(RARE MIGRANT)
DKT
LS

BROAD BORDERED BEE HAWK MOTH (1983)
(Hemaris fuciformis)
MAY – JUNE
FP. HONEYSUCKLE
(DAY FLYING)
NOW A VERY RARE MIGRANT IN THE COUNTY
LS

CONVOLVULUS HAWKMOTH (1972)

(Agrius convolvuli)
JUNE – DEC LARGEST NUMBERS FROM
AUG – NOV.
FP. FIELD BINDWEED, HEDGE BINDWEED.
(SCARCE MIGRANT)
LS

DEATH'S HEAD HAWK MOTH
(1973)
(Acherontia atropus)
LATE AUG – OCT.
FP. POTATO, DEADLY NIGHTSHADE
(RARE MIGRANT)
1/2 LS

ELEPHANT HAWK MOTH (1991)

(Deilephila elpenor)
MAY – JULY.
FP. WILLOW HERBS, FUCHSIA
(DKT)
COMMON
LS

EYED HAWKMOTH (1980)
(Smerinthus ocellata)
MAY – JUNE.
F.P. WILLOW, SALLOW AND APPLE.
(COMMON)
3/4 LS

HUMMINGBIRD HAWKMOTH
(1984)
(Macro glossum stellatarum)
MAY – OCT.
F.P. BEDSTRAWS, WILD MADDER.
(DAY FLYING)
(COMMON MIGRANT)
2 X LS

LIME HAWKMOTH (1979)
(Mimas tiliae)
MAY – JULY.
F.P. LIME, ALDER
(COMMON)
LS

PINE HAWKMOTH (1978)

(Hyloicus pinastri)
JUNE – AUG.
FP. SCOTS PINE, NORWAY SPRUCE.
(LOCAL)
LS

POPLAR HAWKMOTH (1981)

(Laothoe populi)
MAY – JULY
FP. POPLAR, SALLOW AND WILLOW
(COMMON)
3/4 LS

PRIVET HAWKMOTH (1976)

(Sphinx ligustri)
JUNE – JULY.
FP. PRIVET, LILAC
(LOCAL)
3/4 LS

SMALL ELEPHANT HAWKMOTH (1992)
(Deilephila porcellus)
MAY – JULY.
FP. BEDSTRAWS.
(DKT)
(LOCAL)
LS

STRIPED HAWKMOTH (1990) (Hyles lineata)
MAY – OCT.
FP. HEDGE BEDSTRAW (DKT)
(RARE MIGRANT)
3/4 LS

CAN BE FOUND NEARLY EVERYWHERE FROM MAY – SEPT.

It is a scavenging insect and despite the male's scorpion-like tail is completely harmless.

SCORPIONFLY
(Panorpa communis)
THE MALES ABDOMEN IS
SHAPED LIKE A SCORPION'S
TAIL. IT IS NOT A STING, BUT
A GENITAL CAPSULE TIPPED
WITH A CLAW USED TO
HOLD THE FEMALE WHILE
MATING. THE BEAK-LIKE HEAD
IS USED FOR FEEDING.
WINGSPAN: 32MM
2 X LS
(COMMON)

THE FEMALE'S ABDOMEN TAPERS TO A POINT
AT THE REAR. AS PART OF THEIR COURTSHIP
SHE IS OFFERED A DROP OF SALIVA WHICH
THE MALE PLACES ON A LEAF NEAR HER.
LENGTH: 10 – 15MM
2 X LS
(COMMON)

ORDER MEGALOPTERA : ALDERFLIES

ALDERFLIES ARE CLOSELY RELATED TO LACEWINGS.

They can be recognised by their smoky wings and dark veins. They grow up in water, the larvae feeding on other invertebrates. They breathe by way of feather-like gills.

ALDERFLY
(Sialis lutaria)
DESPITE ITS NAME, THERE IS NO DIRECT CONNECTION BETWEEN ALDERFLIES AND ALDER TREES. MAINLY FOUND NEAR LAKES, THE TRANSPARENT STRONGLY VEINED WINGS, FREE OF HAIRS, DISTINGUISH IT FROM THE CADDISFLY. IT IS FOUND WITH THE WINGS FOLDED TENT-WISE OVER THE HEAVY BODY.
WINGSPAN: 35MM
FLIGHT: EARLY SUMMER
2 X LS

ORDER NEUROPTERA : LACEWINGS

SOFT-BODIED, GREEN OR BROWN WITH NUMEROUS DELICATE WING VEINS.

The wings are held over the body at rest. They are carnivorous with the adults and larvae devouring large amounts of aphids.

GREEN LACEWING
(Chrysopa carnea)
THIS SPECIES SPENDS THE WINTER AS AN ADULT OFTEN IN HOUSES, WHERE IT'S PALE GREEN COLOURING CHANGES TO DRAB BROWN. IN SPRING THE GREEN COLOUR RETURNS AS IT BECOMES ACTIVE AGAIN. IT HAS LONG ANTENNAE AND LARGE WINGS, COVERED BY A LACEWORK OF VEINS. SEEN IN LATE SPRING AND SUMMER, IT RARELY FLYS BY DAY UNLESS DISTURBED FROM VEGETATION.
WINGSPAN: 30MM
LENGTH: 15MM
1 1/2 X LS

DRAGONFLIES HAVE BEEN ON EARTH FOR MILLIONS OF YEARS.
THE FIRST INSECT THAT COULD BE RECOGNISED AS A TRUE
DRAGONFLY APPEARED IN A FOSSIL FOUND IN THE PERMIAN AGE SOME,
250 MILLION YEARS AGO.

Generally speaking, Damselflies are small weak fliers, keeping close to
the pondside vegetation and resting with wings close to their bodies.

Dragonflies are much larger, strong fliers often found well away from
water and resting with their wings held at right angles to their bodies.

Both species depend on water for their breeding cycle.
The eggs are laid in water, or on plants, in or near water.
On hatching, the larva spends from a few weeks to 2 years feeding
on other fresh water invertebrates, before emerging to undergo a
final moult into the winged insect.

AZURE DAMSELFLY

(Coenagrion Puella)
FOUND IN A WIDE RANGE OF
WATER SITES USUALLY
PREFERING SMALLER,
SHELTERED PONDS
INCLUDING GARDENS.
WINGSPAN: 38MM
FLIGHT: JUNE - LATE AUG
2 X LS

BANDED DEMOISELLE

(Calopteryx splendens)
FOUND NEAR SLOW-
FLOWING MUD-BOTTOM
STREAMS, RIVERS AND
CANALS WITH OPEN
BANKSIDES AND ADJOINING
MEADOWS.
JUNE - SEPT.
1/2 LS

♂

BANDED DEMOISELLE 1/2 LS

BROWN HAWKER

(Aeshna grandis)
FOUND IN GARDEN PONDS, DYKES, LAKES,
CANALS, SLOW-FLOWING RIVERS, GRAVEL PITS
AND PARK PONDS.
JUNE – OCT.
1/2 LS

BROAD-BODIED CHASER

139

(Libellula depressa)
FOUND IN A WIDE VARIETY
OF STANDING WATER SITES,
FAVOURING SMALL OPEN
PONDS AND DITCHES.
LATE MAY - EARLY AUG.
1/2 LS

BROAD-BODIED CHASER 1/2 LS

COMMON BLUE DAMSELFLY

(Enallagma cyathigerum)
FOUND IN A GREAT VARIETY
OF HABITATS, INCLUDING
GRAVEL PITS, LAKES, PONDS,
AND SLOW RIVERS.
MAY - SEPT.
3/4 LS

COMMON DARTER
(Sympetrum striolatom)
CAN BE FOUND IN A WIDE
RANGE OF WATERBODIES,
FROM PONDS, AND LAKES TO
DITCHES AND RIVERS.
MID-JUNE – NOV.
3/4 LS

FOUR SPOTTED CHASER
(Libellula quadrimaculata)
OCCURS IN A WIDE RANGE
OF HABITATS, INCLUDING
HEATHLAND, MOORLAND
BOGS, FENS, CANALS AND
SLOW-FLOWING STREAMS.
JUNE – AUG.
1/2 LS

HAIRY DRAGONFLY
(Brachyton pratense)
FOUND IN MANY TYPES OF
CLEAN, STILL WATER BODIES
SUCH AS DITCHES, DYKES
AND CANALS.
EARLY MAY – JUNE.
1/2 LS

MIGRANT HAWKER

(Aeshna mixta)
FOUND IN PONDS, LAKES,
GRAVEL-PITS, CANALS AND
SLOW-MOVING RIVERS.
LATE JULY - SEPT.
¹/₂ LS

RED-EYED DAMSELFLY

(Erythromma najas)
FOUND IN STILL-WATER
HABITATS WITH FLOATING
VEGETATION. ALSO IN
SLOW-MOVING RIVERS AND
CANALS WHERE WATER LILIES
AND SIMILAR FLOATING
LEAVED PLANTS GROW.
MID MAY - EARLY JUNE
LS

RED-EYED DAMSELFLY LS

RUDDY DARTER

(Sympetrum sanguineum)
THIS SPECIES PREFERS
SHALLOW, WELL VEGETATED
PONDS, LAKES, CANALS,
BOGGY POOLS AND
DITCHES.
FLIGHT: JULY - SEPT
LS

ORDER OPILIONES : COMMON WOODLOUSE

COMMON WOODLOUSE

(Oniscus asellus)
A VERY COMMON CREATURE
FOUND IN DAMP PLACES*.
THEY FEED AT NIGHT AND
DURING THE DAY, SHELTER
AMONG PLANT LITTER AND
UNDER LOGS AND STONES.

LENGTH: 15MM
$2^{1}/_{2}$ x LS
*AS WOODLICE HAVE 7 PAIRS OF LEGS
THEY ARE NOT CLASSED AS AN INSECT.

ORDER THYSANURA : SILVER FISH

SILVERFISH

(Lepisma saccharina)
THIS IS A SMALL ORDER OF
WINGLESS INSECTS WHICH
HAVE A COATING OF SHINY
SCALES, AND THREE SLENDER
TAILS AT THE REAR. THEY LIVE
IN MOST OF OUR HOMES
EATING A VARIETY OF
STARCHY MATERIALS,
COMMON IN KITCHENS.
LENGTH: 15MM
2 X LS

THE NAME OF ORTHOPTERA MEANS `STRAIGHT-WINGED' AND REFERS
TO THE WAY THE WINGS LAY STRAIGHT BACK ALONG THE BODY.

Grasshoppers are Vegetarians and have short antennae, whereas Crickets are
Omnivorous and have thread-like antennae usually much longer than their
body. The insects are known for their songs. Grasshoppers rub their legs
against their wings whereas Crickets rub their wings together.

COMMON FIELD GRASSHOPPER

(Chorthippus brunneus)
THE SPECIES INHABITS SHORT
TURF OR STONY GROUND
WHERE IT IS HOT AND
SUNNY. CAN ALSO BE
FOUND ALONG ROADSIDE
VERGES. JUNE – NOV.
LENGTH: 20MM
4 X LS

DARK BUSH CRICKET

(Pholidoptera griseoaptera)
CAN BE FOUND IN
HEDGEROWS, WOODLAND
EDGES, NETTLE BEDS,
DITCHES AND OTHER
SUNNY, SHELTERED SITES.
JULY – NOV.
LENGTH: 20MM
4 X LS

ROSSEL'S BUSH CRICKET

(Metrioptera roeselii)
A MEDIUM SIZED CRICKET WITH
WINGS THAT DO NOT USUALLY
REACH THE TIP OF THE
ABDOMEN. FOUND IN ROUGH,
UNGRAZED GRASSLAND AND
SCRUB. JUNE – OCT.
LENGTH: 14 - 21MM
LS

OAK BUSH CRICKET

(Meconema thalassinum)
A SMALL BUSH CRICKET WITH YELLOW AND BROWN MARKINGS ON ITS UPPERSIDE FOUND MAINLY IN OAK WOODS.
MAY – OCT.
LENGTH - 16MM
2 X LS

ORDER TRICHOPTERA :
CADDISFLIES

CADDISFLY
(Halesus radiatus)
THE FOREWINGS OF THIS SPECIES HAVE A PATTERN OF STREAKS AND BLOTCHES WITH RADIATING STREAKS LIKE FINGERS NEAR THE TIP OF THE WINGS. FOUND NEAR RUNNING WATER.
AUG – NOV.
LENGTH: 20MM
2 X LS

LICHENS

LICHENS ARE STABLE, CONSISTENT AND IDENTIFIABLE COMBINATIONS BETWEEN ALGAE AND/OR CYANOBACTERIA AND A FUNGUS.

They are used to indicate whether the air is polluted as they will not tolerate dirty air.

The following are a few examples of lichens of the more well known types found on walls, pavements and church gravestones.

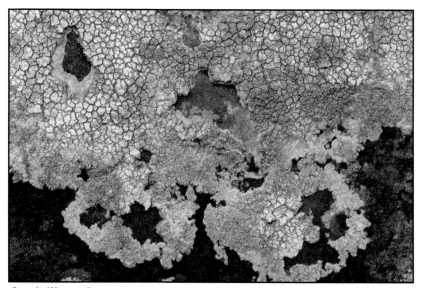

Aspicilla calcarea
HABITAT - COMMON ON HARD CALCAREOUS ROCKS, WALLS AND TOMBSTONES.

Caldonia pyxidata
HABITAT - VERY COMMON, ON MOSSY TREES, ROCKS AND WALLS, OFTEN ON DRIER, MORE SANDY SOILS.

Caloplaca teicholyta
HABITAT - COMMON IN THE SOUTH EAST, MAINLY ON CALCAREOUS SUBSTRATAS ESPECIALLY TOPS OF CHEST-TOMBS.

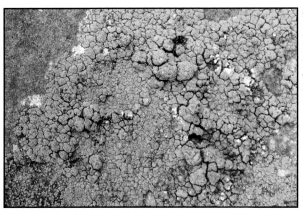

Candelariella vitellina
HABITAT - COMMON ON NUTRIENT - ENRICHED SILICEOUS ROCKS, ESPECIALLY THOSE FREQUENTED BY BIRDS.

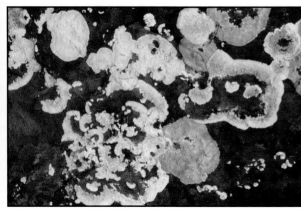

Diploica canescens

HABITATS - VERY COMMON
ON BASIC AND VERY
NUTRIENT - ENRICHED
TREES, ROCKS AND WALLS,
SUCH AS FARMYARD
BUILDINGS.

Evernia prunastri

HABITAT - VERY COMMON
ON DECIDUOUS TREES,
RARELY ON ROCKS, FENCE
POSTS AND SAND DUNES.

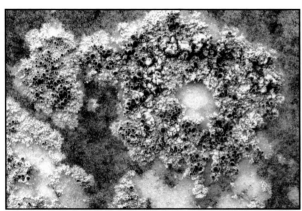

Lecanora campestris

HABITAT - VERY COMMON
ON TOMBSTONES AND
WALLS.

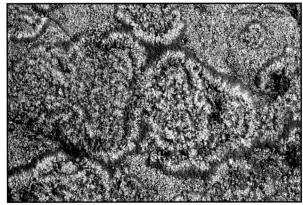

Lecanulata dispersa

HABITAT - VERY COMMON
VERY POLLUTION RESISTANT
AND FOUND EVEN IN
CITY CENTRES ON
NUTRIENT-RICH BASIC
SUBSTRATES.

Lecanora muralis

HABITAT - VERY COMMON
ON MAN-MADE SUBSTRATES
INCUDING PAVING STONES
& ASPHALT.

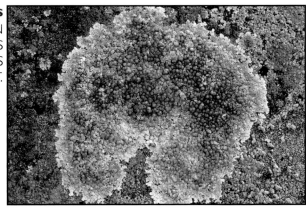

Physcia caesia

HABITAT - VERY COMMON
ON NUTRIENT - ENRICHED
ROCKS, ASBESTOS - CEMENT,
ASPHALT, AND TOMBSTONES.

Psilolechia lucida
HABITAT - VERY COMMON
ON SHADED ROCKS AND
BRICKS ESPECIALLY WHERE IT
IS DAMP, NOT NORMALLY
FOUND ON TREES.

Tephromela atra
HABITAT - VERY COMMON
ON WELL-LIT SILICEOUS
ROCKS AND WALLS, RARELY
FOUND ON TREES.

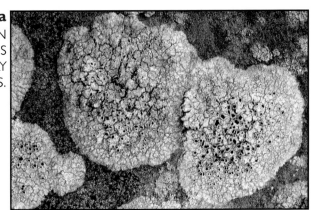

Xanthoria parietina
HABITAT - VERY COMMON
ON NUTRIENT-RICH TREES,
ROCKS AND WALLS,
ESPECIALLY BIRD-PERCHING
SITES, ON ROOFS UNDER
TELEVISION AERIALS.

MISCELLANEOUS SECTION

DARK-LIPPED BANDED SNAIL

(Cepaea nemoralis)

FIVE DARK BANDS ARE COMMON BUT NOT ALWAYS PRESENT. THE NUMBER AND SPACING OF THE BANDS AND COLOUR CAN HAVE MANY VARIATIONS. THEY ARE FOUND IN HEDGES AND GRASSY PLACES.
SHELL SIZE: 22MM WIDE X 25MM HIGH

RAMSHORN WATER SNAIL

FOUND IN LARGE BODIES OF HARD WATER AREAS THROUGHOUT THE COUNTY.

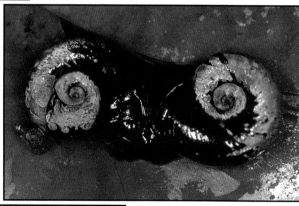

LEOPARD SLUG

(Limax maximus)

THIS SLUG IS MAINLY FOUND IN DAMP WOODLANDS, THROUGHOUT THE COUNTY.
LENGTH: 70MM

GREAT CRESTED NEWT

(Triturus cristatus)
WARTY LUMPS COVER THE DARK BROWN, BLOTCHY SKIN. MALES HAVE A SILVER STREAK ON THE TAIL AND AT BREEDING TIME DEVELOP HIGH CRINKLED CREST, SEPARATE FROM THE TAILCREST AND A BRIGHT ORANGE BELLY. THE FEMALE HAS NO CREST.
LENGTH: 16.5CM (FEMALE)
(THIS IS A PROTECTED SPECIES).

PALMATE NEWT

(Triturus helveticus)
THIS IS THE SMALLEST OF OUR THREE NATIVE SPECIES. THEY MOVE FROM HIBERNATION NOOKS ON LAND TO BREED IN SMALL WATER AREAS. THE OLIVE-BROWN UNDER PARTS ARE NOT SPOTTED BUT THERE IS USUALLY A DARK STREAK ACROSS THE EYE. MALES AT BREEDING TIME HAVE WEBBED HIND FEET.
LENGTH: 75MM

SMOOTH NEWT

(Triturus vulgaris)
THIS NEWT IS THE MOST WIDESPREAD OF THE BRITISH NEWTS.
THE MALE HAS A LOW RIDGE OF SKIN RUNNING ALONG ITS BACK IN SUMMER. THE REMAINS OF ITS SPRING BREEDING CREST.
LENGTH: 10CM

COMMON FROG
(Rana temporaria)
CONTRARY TO POPULAR BELIEF, COMMON
FROGS SPEND MOST OF THEIR LIVES ON THE
LAND. BETWEEN JAN – MARCH THEY GATHER
IN SHALLOW PONDS TO SPAWN.
FROGS HAVE A SMOOTH, MOIST SKIN AND
MOVE BY SPRINGY LEAPS.
THE FEMALE GROWS TO 75MM LONG.

FROG TADPOLE
(BETWEEN 7-12 WEEKS)

COMMON TOAD
(Bufo bufo)
THE TOAD DIFFERS FROM
THE FROG IN HAVING A
DRIER WARTY SKIN, A LARGE
GLAND BEHIND THE EYE
AND SHORTER LEGS
ON WHICH THEY DO NOT
HOP BUT CRAWL.
FEMALES OUT-GROW
THE MALES AND MAY REACH
10CM LONG.

OTTER

(Lutra lutra)
THE OTTER IS STREAMLINED
FOR SPEED IN THE WATER.
IT HAS SMALL EARS, A LONG
BODY AND POWERFUL
TAPERING TAIL, SHORT LEGS
WHICH ARE WEBBED.
IT HAS RECENTLY BEEN
INTRODUCED BACK INTO
THE COUNTY.
(THIS IS A PROTECTED SPECIES).

GRASS SNAKE

(Natrix natrix)
THIS IS BRITAIN'S LARGEST
AND COMMONEST SNAKE.
IT CAN BE FOUND IN DAMP
GRASS, DITCHES, POND
BANKS AND SLOW MOVING
STREAMS. IT OFTEN FEEDS IN
THE EARLY MORNING AND A
LARGE MEAL WILL SATISFY IT
FOR A WEEK OR TEN DAYS.
IT HIBERNATES AT THE
BEGINNING OF OCT. IN WALL
CREVICES, UNDER TREE
ROOTS OR IN SIMILAR PLACES.
LENGTH: 120CM (FEMALE).

SLOW-WORM

(Anguis fragilis)
SLOW-WORMS ARE SLEEK,
SHINY, SNAKE-LIKE LIZARDS.
ADULTS VARY IN COLOUR
FROM GREYISH TO LIGHT,
DARK OR COPPERY BROWN.
THEY LIVE ON SUNNY BANKS
AND HILLSIDES WHERE THERE
IS GOOD COVER OF GRASS.
HIBERNATION UNDERGROUND
BEGINS IN OCT. AND ENDS IN
MARCH.
LENGTH: 45CM

BROWN RAT
(Rattus norvegicus)
THE BROWN (OR COMMON RAT) WILL EAT NEARLY ANYTHING AND THRIVES WHERE THERE ARE FOOD STORES OR WASTE.
IT HAS COARSE GREY-BROWN FUR, SMALL FINELY HAIRED EARS AND A THICK SCALY TAIL.
LENGTH: 28CM (MALE)
23CM (FEMALE)

COMMON SHREW
(Sorex araneus)
SHREWS USE UP SO MUCH ENERGY THAT THEY HAVE TO EAT FREQUENTLY. THEY ARE BOTH ACTIVE IN THE DAYTIME AS WELL AS AT NIGHT.
LENGTH: (HEAD & BODY) 75MM

FIELD VOLE
(Microtus agrestis)
OVERGROWN FIELDS AND PLACES WITH LONG ROUGH GRASS ARE TYPICALLY WHERE YOU CAN FIND THIS ANIMAL.
THE NORMAL LIFE SPAN IS ONLY ABOUT ONE YEAR.
LENGTH: (HEAD & BODY) 10CM

HARVEST MOUSE

(Micromys minutus)
ONE OF THE WORLD'S SMALLEST
RODENTS, WEIGHING LESS THAN
A 2P COIN.
ITS BLUNT NOSE, SMALLER EARS AND
YELLOW-BROWN FUR DISTINGUISH
THE TINY, AGILE HARVEST MOUSE,
WHICH LIVES AMONG TALL STIFF-
STEMMED VEGETATION AND USES ITS
TAIL AS A FIFTH LIMB TO GRASP STALKS.
LENGTH: (HEAD & BODY) 64MM. LS

WOOD MOUSE

(Apodemus sylvaticus)
WIDESPREAD IN ALL TYPES OF
HABITATS FROM WOODLANDS TO
SAND DUNES AND GARDENS.
IT'S SANDY-BROWN COAT AND
LARGE EARS AND EYES HELP TO
DISTINGUISH THE WOOD MOUSE.
THE UNDER PARTS ARE WHITE WITH
A YELLOW STREAK ON THE CHEST
AND THE TAIL IS LIGHTLY HAIRED.
LENGTH: (HEAD & BODY) 95MM

WEASEL

(Mustela nivalis)
THIS IS THE SMALLEST BRITISH CARNIVORE
AND IS FAST-MOVING. A FIERCE HUNTER
BY DAY OR NIGHT, MICE ARE ONE OF ITS
MAIN FOODS.
MOST WEASELS DO NOT LIVE TO BE MORE
THAN 1 YEAR OLD. THEIR LITTER IS USUALLY
FIVE OR SIX.
LENGTH: (HEAD & BODY) 20CM

GREY SQUIRREL
(Sciurus carolinenis)
ONE OF BRITAIN'S MOST
FAMILIAR ANIMALS, IT WAS
INTRODUCED TO THE UK
FROM AMERICA IN THE MID
19TH CENTURY.
IT DOES NOT HIBERNATE
AND CAN BE SEEN FEEDING
ON FINE DAYS DURING
WINTER MONTHS.

FALLOW DEER
(Dama dama)
FALLOW DEER CAN BE SEEN
FEEDING AT ANYTIME, BUT
DAWN AND DUSK ARE
GENERALLY WHEN YOU WILL
SEE THEM IN THE WILD.
RUTTING TAKES PALCE IN
OCT - NOV THE
MATING PERIOD.

MUNTJAC
(Muntiacus reevesi)
THE SMALLEST BRITISH DEER.
IT HAS A GLOSSY
RED-BROWN SUMMER COAT
AND IS DISTINGUISHED BY
ITS RATHER ROUNDED BACK.
THE DOE LACKS ANTLERS
AND CAN BE FOUND IN
WOODLAND AND SCRUB.

HEDGEHOG

(Erinaceus europaeus)
AN ADULT HEDGEHOG HAS
SOME 5000 SPINES ON ITS
BACK. IT'S BRITAINS ONLY
SPINY MAMMAL AND HAS
BEEN FOUND IN GARDENS,
HEDGEROWS AND MEADOWS
FOR CENTURIES.
IT HIBERNATES IN WINTER
AMONG LEAVES AND GRASS
AND LIVES OFF THE BODY FAT
BUILT UP IN THE AUTUMN.
LENGTH: 25CM

PIPISTRELLE BAT

(Pipistrellus pipistrellus)
THIS IS BRITAIN'S SMALLEST BAT AND WILL
CONGREGATE IN LARGE COLONIES OFTEN IN
BUILDINGS SUCH AS CHURCHES.
THEY HIBERNATE FROM LATE NOV. TO LATE
MARCH.
LENGTH: 35MM
LS

RABBIT

(Oryctolagus cuniculus)
IT WAS THE 12TH CENTURY BEFORE THE
RABBIT APPEARED IN BRITAIN, HAVING BEEN
INTRODUCED FROM THE CONTINENT AS A
VALUABLE SOURCE OF MEAT AND SKINS.
LENGTH: 48CM

BADGER

(Meles meles)

THE BADGER EMERGES CAUTIOUSLY FROM IT'S SETT, SNIFFING FOR
DANGER SOON AFTER DUSK. IT HAS VERY STRONG FRONT PAWS
WITH LONG CLAWS WHICH MAKES IT A POWERFUL DIGGER. ITS MAIN
FOOD IS EARTHWORMS, BUT WILL ALSO EAT FALLEN FRUIT, CEREALS,
BEETLES AND SOME MAMMALS INCLUDING YOUNG RABBITS.
LENGTH: (HEAD & BODY) 76CM MALE

SPIDERS ARE REGARDED BY PEOPLE IN WIDELY DIFFERING WAYS, THIS MAY BE FEAR, HATRED OR ADMIRATION.

Spiders are predatory, carnivorous Arthropods with their prey being largely consisting of insects. Spiders have eight hollow legs and a two part body. The abdomen (the hind part) is soft, the front part has an upper shell of armour called the Carapace and the underneath, a shell called the Sternum.

Araneus diadematus

THE FEMALE HAS A WHITE CROSS ON HER BACK, THE MALE IS ONLY ABOUT A QUARTER SIZE OF THE FEMALE AND DOES NOT SHARE HER WEB, BUT SCAVENGES OFF IT.

Dysdera crocata

THIS REDDISH IMPRESSIVE LOOKING SPIDER IS NOCTURNAL, SPENDING THE DAYTIME IN A SILKEN CELL IN WHICH THE FEMALE LAYS HER EGGS. CAN BE FOUND UNDER STONES, LOGS AND OTHER DEBRIS.

Micromata virescens

BOTH SEXES HAVE A GREEN APPEARANCE. THEY CATCH THEIR PREY BY WAITING AND GRABBING RATHER THAN BY PURSUIT. (RARE FOR COUNTY).

Scotophaeus blackwalli

THIS SPECIES CAN BE FOUND IN AND AROUND HOUSES, UNDER BARK AND IN HOLES IN WALLS. IT NORMALLY HUNTS AT NIGHT.
LENGTH: 10 – 12MM (FEMALE)

Tibellus oblongus

THIS SPIDER HAS AN ELONGATED APPEARANCE AND HAS THE HABIT OF EXTENDING ITS LEGS. THEY CATCH THEIR PREY BY AMBUSHING PASSING INSECTS. FOUND IN DAMP INLAND HABITATS.
LENGTH 8 – 10 MM (FEMALE)

Zelotes latrellei

THE WHOLE SPIDER IS BLACK CAN BE FOUND UNDER STONES AND RAISED PATCHES OF VEGETATION WITHIN MARSHY SITES.
LENGTH: 7 – 8MM (FEMALE)

THE FORCES OF NATURE

LIGHT WE SEE IT BUT CANNOT TOUCH OR HOLD IT
WIND WE FEEL IT BUT CANNOT TOUCH OR HOLD IT

FIRE WE SEE IT, WE CAN FEEL AND TOUCH IT
WATER WE SEE IT WE CAN TOUCH AND HOLD IT
TAKE TIME TO STOP AND STARE

FURTHER READING

- (LICHENS)
  FRANK S. DOBSON
  ISBN 085546 0946

- (SHIELDBUGS & SQUASH BUGS OF THE BRITISH ISLES)
  MARTIN EVANS & ROGER EDMONDSON
  ISBN 0-9549506-0-7

- (GRASSHOPPERS & CRICKETS OF BRITAIN/IRELAND)
  MARTIN EVANS & ROGER EDMONDSON
  ISBN 978-0-9549506-1-3

- (COLLINS COMPLETE BRITISH INSECTS)
  MICHAEL CHINERY
  ISBN 978-0-00-717966-4

- (BUTTERFLIES & DAY FLYING MOTHS OF BRITAIN & EUROPE)
  MICHAEL CHINERY
  ISBN 0-00-219787-1

- (WILD FLOWERS OF BRITAIN & IRELAND)
  MARJORIE BLAMY, RICHARD & ALASTAIR FITTER,
  ISBN 0-7136-59-44-0

- (FIELD GUIDE TO THE BIRDS OF BRITAIN & EUROPE)
  JIM FLEGG'S
  ISBN 1-85368-080-X

- (THE ENCYCLOPEDIA OF FUNGI OF BRITAIN & EUROPE)
  MICHEAL JORDAN
  ISBN 0-7112-2379-3

- (BRITISH PLANT GALLS)
  MARGARET REDFERN & PETER SHIRLEY
  ISBN 1-85153-2145

- (SPIDERS OF BRITAIN & NORTHERN EUROPE)
  MICHAEL J. ROBERTS
  ISBN 0-00-219981-5

- (MOTHS OF GREAT BRITAIN & IRELAND)
  PAUL WARING & MARTIN TOWNSEND
  ISBN 0-9531399-2-1

- BRITISH PYRALID MOTHS
  BARRY GOATER
  ISBN 0-946589-08-9

USEFUL ADDRESSES

THE WILDLIFE TRUST - DESBOROUGH & DISTRICT GROUP
HAZELAND HOUSE
HIGH ST
DESBOROUGH
NORTHANTS

THE WILDLIFE TRUST - FINEDON & DISTRICT GROUP
FINEDON OLD BAND CLUB
ORCHARD RD
FINEDON
NORTHANTS

THE WILDLIFE TRUST FOR NORTHAMPTONSHIRE,
BEDFORDSHIRE & CAMBRIDGESHIRE
LINGS HOUSE
BILLING LINGS
NORTHAMPTON
NN3 8BE

BARNWELL COUNTRY PARK
BARNWELL ROAD
OUNDLE
PETERBOROUGH
NORTHANTS
PE8 5PB

BRIXWORTH COUNTRY PARK & BRAMPTON VALLEY WAY
NORTHAMPTON ROAD
BRIXWORTH
NORTHANTS
NN6 9DG

FERMYN WOODS COUNTRY PARK
LYVEDEN RD
BRIGSTOCK
KETTERING
NORTHANTS
NN14 3HS

IRCHESTER COUNTRY PARK
GYPSY LANE
LITTLE IRCHESTER
NORTHANTS
NN29 7DL

STANWICK LAKES
HIGHAM RD
STANWICK
NORTHANTS
NN9 6GY

SUMMER LEYS NATURE RESERVE
C/O WILDLIFE TRUST
LINGS HOUSE
BILLING LINGS
NORTHAMPTON
NN3 8BE

SYWELL COUNTRY PARK
WASHBROOK LANE
ECTON
NORTHAMPTON
NN6 0QX

R.S.P.B. CENTRE
TOP LODGE
FINESHADE WOOD
NR CORBY
NN17 3BB

KETTERING & DISTRICT NATURAL HISTORY SOCIETY
THE CRESCENTS COMMUNITY CENTRE
LABURNUM CRESCENT
KETTERING
NN16

NORTHAMPTON NATURAL HISTORY SOCIETY
THE HUMFREY ROOMS
10, CASTILLIAN TERRACE
NORTHAMPTON
NN1 1LD

ACKNOWLEDGMENTS

The Author would like to thank the following for their help in producing this book.

Mrs Juliette Butler (Wildlife Trust Northampton), Mrs Gill Gent (Flowers, Northants Recorder), Mr Jack Laundon (Lichens), Mr D. Manning (Galls, Northants Recorder), Mr John Showers (Insects, Northants Recorder), Mr Jake Ward (Birds), Mr Michael Wallis, Mr Jeff Blincow (Fungi, Northants Recorder) and Mr Tony White (Spiders, Northants Recorder).

A special thanks to the group 'Wild Bunch' led by Mr Tony Richardson (Compton Estate Conservation Officer). I have enjoyed the members company over many years and through them have been able to visit areas within the county which I would not normally have been able to on my own.

All the above have provided valuable information, however, responsibility for all errors and omissions remains in my court.

Mr Roger Barker for scanning all the pictures on to CD's for the printers to use in making this publication possible.

PHOTOGRAPHY

With the exception of the Red Kite which is by Derek Henderson, who has kindly agreed that I can reproduce his image in this book.

All other pictures have been taken by the Author using - Nikon 35mm Film and Leica Digital Cameras.

D. Larkin
26/5/10.